NOREN

暖簾

Photography and design by Tadashi Masuda

The Design Heritage of Noren
—Traditional Japanese Storefront Art—

Published by Graphic-sha Publishing Co., Ltd.
1-9-12 Kudankita, Chiyoda-ku, Tokyo, Japan.

Distributors:
UNITED STATES: Kodansha International/USA, Ltd., through Harper & Row, Publishers, Inc., 10 East 53rd Street, New York, N.Y. 10022. SOUTH AMERICA: Harper & Row, Publishers, Inc., International Department. CANADA: Fitzhenry & Whiteside Ltd., 195 Allstate Parkway, Markham, Ontario L3R 4T8. MEXICO AND CENTRAL AMERICA: HARLA S.A. de C.V., Apartado 30-546, Mexico 4, D.F. BRITISH ISLES: Premier Book Marketing Ltd., 1 Gower Street, London WC1E 6HA. EUROPEAN CONTINENT: European Book Service PBD, Strijkviertel 63, 3454 PK DE MEERN, The Netherlands. Australia and New Zealand: Bookwise International, 54 Crittenden Road, Findon, South Australia 5007. THE FAR EAST: Japan Publications Trading Co., 1-2-1, Sarugaku-cho, Chiyoda-ku, Tokyo 101.

First Printing: January 1989
ISBN 0-87040-770-8

Printed in Japan

CONTENTS

Noren Pilgrimage by Taro Yamamoto — 7
Praises to Noren by Yoshio Hayakawa — 10
The Noren and I by Tadashi Masuda — 14
Tohaku District — 17
Kanto District — 29
Hokuriku District — 47
Chubu District — 63
Kinki District — 85
Chugoku District — 153
Shikoku District — 161
Kyushu District — 167
Kana-syllable Index — 179

Noren Pilgrimage

Taro Yamamoto
(Poet)

The number of *noren* that Tadashi Masuda photographed over a ten year period was immense. As I looked over the selected photographs I ruminated, attempting to understand what he was searching for on his frequent expeditions.

Thick files were piled up on the desk and from among them unique and extraordinary brown and indigo dyed *noren* appeared one after the other. They varied from *noren* hanging under eaves to awning *noren* and gorgeous bridal *noren* that were part of the bride's trousseau and resembled the long, traditional Japanese kimono *uchikake* overcoat. There were various other kinds such as the plain and simple ones adorning old-fashioned shops that I remembered seeing occasionally on trips. The depth of the *noren* pilgrimage over a ten-year period was truly prodigious and I was awed by it. However, I kept asking myself, "What is he trying to capture?"

In 1977, Masuda's first exhibit called "Walls, Windows, and Doors" taken over a twenty-year period was the talk of the town. The photographs displayed under the subheading "Expressions of Life" at that time were all taken overseas.

In a small piece he wrote for a magazine that featured this exhibition, I found that Masuda photographed with an insatiable vigor probing not only into the Japanese home but also combing the streets of foreign cities for twenty long years without losing interest. Rather than poring over prints at a desk, he worked his whole body into a sweat like a hunter of beauty closing in on his subjects to the very end. Looking at this series of *noren*, I could visualize him with several cameras thrown over his shoulder, stalking his subjects intently.

Despite his busy schedule, he made time on the weekends for his shooting expeditions, which, however, frequently proved fruitless. *Noren* were already objects of the past and quickly disappearing from the entrances of shops and homes. When I described him as a hunter, I did not mean to insinuate he plunged into things blindly or recklessly. Before going out on an expedition, every detail concerning his destination and the nature of the locality was investigated and the target was decided. Of course, in reality things did not always go as planned, and there were gaps in the schedule. For instance, even when there was a superb *noren* and the history of the shop had been thoroughly studied, permission to photograph might be denied.

On the other hand, there were times when he came across the prize of the expedition, a completely unexpected discovery. The series "Walls, Windows, and Doors" was another collection of these discoveries. It is a great joy to see those wonderful old structures built long ago still standing proudly today, such places as the nameless *dangoya* (dumpling shop) and the tea shop on the summit. The joy of Masuda's discovery, captured through his lens, is conveyed directly to us. This makes the photo collection so especially rich and thoroughly enjoyable.

For the time being, everything concerning the question "What is he trying to capture?" was tucked away in my mind, and to recall it again I just close my eyes. Masterpieces are always silent about themselves, but if you listen carefully, I think you can hear their stories.

As an object, what is a *noren*? The symbolism in the *noren* design which is simplified to its basic essence must appeal to the designer. The *noren*, so to speak, personifies "the face" or prestige of the shop. It must present the trade of the shop in an explicit and clear manner. The realism in the trademark and store name is the result of reality being condensed to its ultimate form, and thus giving birth to abstract beauty. There is no denying the magnetism and charm the *noren* possesses. It is not unlikely that Masuda's work up to now, which dealt with so many symbols, is fundamentally related to his *noren* expeditions.

Is that all there is to *noren*? No, there are more intricate aspects, as well. While centering on the *noren*, most of Masuda's work also expertly captures the mood of the surroundings, the lattice and window, the back entrance and room interior, and so forth. The word *noren* originated in China and was introduced into Japan with the Zen sect of Buddhism. In ancient times it was called *tobari* and used during the 14th century as a room divider like a *shoji* screen and *fusuma* sliding door. It was during 16th century with the emergence of the powerful merchant class that it began to appear in front of houses. Symbols were probably incorporated at this time. While doing historical reseach on the *noren*, Masuda may have also wanted to examine continuous changes in the Japanese house and its spatial configuration.

Although the abstract and traditional beauty of the *noren* have been discussed, his work also imparts the darker side of the *noren*. Masuda states, "There is still an overwhelmingly large number of *noren* in Kyoto. Clinging to the old, Kyoto still inherently embraces a closed society where tradition is strongly visible in the shop signs."

I do not think he was merely carried away by the refined beauty of the quaint shops and their *noren*. Behind the tranquil exterior of ancient houses going back five, six or many more generations are hidden violent dramas of life. As proof of this, such phrases come to mind: "disgrace the *noren*", "protect the *noren*", and "stake your life on the *noren*".

The custom of sharing the *noren*, "*Noren Wake*", is fading away now. Many forces are involved. First is the old established house going back many generations that shares the *noren*. Second is the side with whom it shared, resembling the situation of a branch shop to a main shop. Lastly, are the workmen who are not given the honor to share the *noren* and are employed in service for life. There may have been some blood feuds to "protect the *noren*" which can be traced back for generations and which are still going on today. Another ominous trait of old, established houses, irrespective of locality, is their homogeneity. In addition, the tradition of the merchant class in Japan based on a law of realism different from that of the *samurai* is firmly observed.

On the other hand, I can not help but think of the saying "*noren ni udeoshi*" that is said by children, as well. This is a common phrase used by the general populace against an established *noren* house. The opposition consists of the people who are desperately trying to "protect the *noren*", and they are against the side earnestly trying to put up a new *noren*. There are probably many subcontractors crying under the silent pressure of one *noren*. An example is the relationship between the wholesale dealer and the cheap labor dyers of Yūzen silk.

The *noren* is undeniably beautiful and graceful, giving entrances an aura of prominence and power. However, looking deeply into Masuda's work, I believe the *noren* he portrays are a hidden testimony of the conservatism in the merchant class in Japan that cannot be eradicated.

Among the *noren* in the files, there are some that have become old and ragged from the touch and sweat of people passing under them. A bit of exaggeration perhaps, but I think they may also be stained with blood. If one can not sense such dramas behind the *noren*, then, what was the purpose of the ten years Tadashi Masuda invested in *Noren* pilgrimage? However, those who are zealous collectors of objects cannot be expected to see the "body and soul" of *noren* without the same dedicated effort as Masuda's.

Praises to Noren

Yoshio Hayakawa
(Graphic designer)

In 1978, when I was walking along the back streets of Cairo on my first trip to Egypt, a foul smell drifted in the air as bizarrely dressed crowds swarmed over the unpaved ground. Just then, the story Tadashi Masuda had told me before I departed for Egypt came to me. It had happened twenty years ago. While he was wandering here and there on his new expedition photographing private homes in Cairo, he found himself surrounded by ten men clambering for a tip. Feeling himself in danger, he ran away in a frenzy.

From there my journey took me from Cairo to Luxor, Aswan and upstream along the Nile where I visited the age-old buildings and sculptures of ancient Egypt. During that time my mind kept making comparisons throughout the journey in Egypt with the environment in Japan which was symbolized in this already commissioned essay. I tried to conceive the image of *noren* amidst the drab Cairo streets and the giant temple pillars towering in the desert but to no avail. The two conflicting images were unmatched. While Masuda was continuing his photographing inside and outside Japan, I wondered how he was going to combine the two.

Almost every Friday night for ten years he waited impatiently for his work to finish at the Institute; then he could take off lugging his heavy camera equipment over his shoulders. During the following two days he traveled to numerous towns and places as far away as Kyushu, Shikoku, and even Tohoku districts. Making previous arrangements at the places he would visit, he hired a local taxi and searched for old houses and their *noren* to photograph them. After making his rounds during the two-day period, Saturday and Sunday, he returned to Tokyo early Monday morning.

The *noren*, which is no more than a piece of cloth with an emblem on one side, has fluttered for ages against the wind and snow. One particular trait in the everyday life of traditional Japan, it has functioned as a light screen separating the interior world from the exterior or as a trademark representing the family house of a shop. In addition to its role in everyday life, it is graceful and serene, adding an indescribable charm to houses and towns.

What motive prompted Masuda to try to capture the mystique of *noren* ? From the aspect of beauty you could probably cite the interesting traditional designs made up of simple symbols dyed on pieces of cloth. His fanatic devotion in spending almost all of his holidays and energy on this work was most likely due to his realization of the difficulty of the *noren* surviving in today's world. He saw its motifs disappearing before his eyes. His motive, then, was his love for a dying art form.

He said, "I wanted to photograph this place again, but when I went to the house I had previously called at the year before the dwelling had been rebuilt with modern building material. A plastic signboard was hanging in front."

Regardless of city or district, the tranquil, pure pre-Edo style is becoming rarer in our rapidly changing Japanese towns and cities. You would think the perfect harmony created by the natural building materials of wood, mud plaster, grass, and paper bestowed on us by Nature would be preserved. I remember a comment by the critic Shinichi Kusamori in a newspaper I read saying that when he looked out the window of a Bullet train he saw only the aluminum sash shining around the window pane and *shoji*-door of a thatch-roofed house. Upon this sight he declared that he would never use aluminum sash.

Aside from the old houses and streets preserved in Kyoto and Kanazawa, the original wood and mud-plaster walls are not reused when ordinary houses are rebuilt. No doubt new manufactured modern building materials such as aluminum sash and plastic are employed. From the fundamental point of economics and convenience in everyday living this cannot be helped. As opposed to the aesthetics of stone in Europe, the refined elegance of Japanese natural building material is vanishing day by day. *Noren* in its entirety can be considered as one of the dying traditions. Nowadays, with the wide use of synthetic materials, there is no chance of *noren* making a comeback.

Masuda feels sympathy and sorrow for the disappearance of such things. Not merely intangible reflections of the mind, the *noren* has a definite "shape" in the beauty of its design that deeply appeals to the sensitivity of a designer. As though on a kind of mission he has pursued this single subject for ten years.

Tadashi Masuda is not a photographer; he is a graphic designer. However, photographing objects is not the pastime of a designer, nor do the photographs serve as reference material accurately recording the shape, color and quality of the subject. They are autonomous works completed by Masuda, whose technique is on a par with that of a professional, with a firm foundation and a fine eye for details.

I would like to explain the real origin of his interest in photography. His dramatic encounter with photography began when he participated in the Graphics Group that engineered a new epoch in postwar-graphics history twenty-five years ago. This new group was made up of the leading photographers and designers of the day. The teamwork by both groups, which involved tough scrimmages and high tension, brought a new sense of aesthetics. This bore fruit in a fresh visual image that won great attention. Belonging to this group, he insatiably devoured all the basic knowledge and technology of photography with an unappeasable appetite. He described his infatuation saying, "Being a perfectionist, I became enthralled with all the magic powers of lenses and emulsions. It was a period when I wanted to put away my palette and remodel my studio to build a darkroom."

Since then he has produced many great great works at the Tadashi Masuda Design Institute that have primarily involved photographic representation. In particular, his series of travel posters of the Ibaraki area has provided a fresh outlook in a stereotyped world.

In addition to the work on *noren*, he has also continued to photograph nameless old houses with extraordinary perseverance for the last twenty years. They number in the thousands. The other day when I visited his studio, I was astonished to find that his many bookshelves lining the walls were jampacked with scrapbooks. In Masuda's case, these were not photographs he just happened to take on his trips. Instead, he went on trips to take them.

In one of the explanations he wrote for students he stated, "Walking around the city I absorbed the sights—such as the window of an old building, a simple scaffold left hanging unobtrusively or a drum can or steel plate discarded close by. After digesting them, I find countless things that are usually invisible and that can lead to some very interesting developments. By the single method of radically cutting off observation and range of vision and extracting the results, the original subject ceases to be and the detail takes on a new life of its own." This is no doubt an extreme statement of Masuda's aesthetics. He is a camera-fiend. He said, "One time while focussing on my subject, I started to lose my balance. Completely engrossed, I continued to move backwards and fell into a small stream holding my camera." He relates his strong, endless desire to continue on this road of photography: "As long I can see and move around and am full of energy, I want to continue this work steadfastly."

The above may seem a little long and overstated, but I would like you to understand the background of Tadashi Masuda's *noren*, that is, his extraordinary character, the accuracy of his eye, and his firm technical expertise. The photographs in Masuda's *noren* produce an invaluable record that covers a wide area comprising over 29 prefectures and Tokyo and extending from the "Snow Country" to southern Japan. He captures the joys and sorrows of the subject and transposes them to photographs. Just before becoming sentimental, he suppresses these feelings and captures the image with a cool and composed eye.

This book does not only sing praises to *noren*. Presenting as many works as circumstances permit, this book could be considered an "encyclopedia." Masuda transmits an aspect of traditional Japan through one genre and portrays it from various angles, compiling it into this beautiful book. Regardless of today's different values, the changes of time and the coming and going of fads, it stands firm as a monument.

In closing, I would like to say that it has been my great pleasure to be a friend of Tadashi Masuda and to be living in the same world as him.

The Noren and I

Tadashi Masuda
(Graphic Designer)

I was surprised by the sudden sight of a new building standing where just awhile ago a plain and simple house once stood. The wave of urbanization is rapidly standardizing the structure and appearance of towns and cities alike. I miss the traditional beauty of old Japanese houses and tiny little shops gradually being hidden in the shadows. These days the nostalgic *noren* is also dwindling in number. Since ancient times the *noren* has signified the "face" or the prestige of shops and stores and is the cultural heritage of the common man.

Withstanding wind and snow and aging with time, the "trademark" *noren* of the common man may seem no more than a piece of cloth. However, it is of great historical significance with each *noren* reflecting the strenuous lifestyle of the merchant and craftman. The *noren* is a unique Japanese custom that symbolizes reliability and trust that cannot be found in the stone and brick culture of the West.

As an example of man's resourcefulness, this piece of cloth first served as a shield against wind and dust. In the beginning of the 16th century it evolved into the "trademark" *noren* of the merchant where it was displayed on storefronts. Its popularity spread from the Medieval Period and upon entering the 18th century it had become the symbolic flag-insignia of the thriving townspeople's spirit.

They ranged from the "trademark" *noren* of shops and stores to utilitarian ones used as screens and room dividers, and to special traditional ones such as the Kaga *noren* of the Hokuriku district and the festival *noren* of the Tohoku district. They varied in dyes, cloth, shapes and use; however they all have one common trait: unique markings.

Their occupational uses are great, ranging from the *dagashi* sweets of the "Snow Country" to the special sweets of the South, from tavern eating houses on Kisoji Road to the Japanese restaurant of Kyoraku, from simple hand-dyed ones to the gorgeous Kyoto Yūzen silk and Nishijin weaves. Simplified objects representing the trade and Japanese characters written in distinct brushstrokes observed in surviving *noren* are the rudiments of today's symbols and logotypes. Formative thinking fostered over the centuries is still active.

The tranquil composure of an old store is deluding. The store seems timeless, as though it has been standing and surviving for generations. From a historical point of view, it is new and insignificant, but in order to come into existence, it had to overcome its predecessors. *Noren* depicts various new and old life styles. Behind the dyed cloth lie hidden, violent dramas of human strife, but at the same time, the *noren* is a precious "testimony of its era."

The cultural heritage of the common man is gradually disappearing. Captivated by the simple and unassuming private homes, the old town houses and the *noren*, I began photographing them and the life surrounding them with the theme of "Walls, Windows, and Doors" in mind, hoping to keep a record through my own eyes.

While photographing for a long time over a wide area I was again impressed most by Kyoto. A thousand-year-old city, with many of its exquisite buildings still standing and time-honored *noren* fluttering in the breeze, it seemed that time had stopped. It is said that the people of Kyoto are lovers of old shops. Depending on the place and time, there is a strangeness in the air that makes it unapproachable to outsiders.

A relatively small number of *noren* that has not been destroyed by wars or fires can also be found in outlying towns. Differing from the *noren* in Kyoto, each is a product of its background, reflecting a warm serenity, a heart yearning for the past, or a simple design characteristic of that area.

When I was in Morioka to do some shooting, the cold winter wind blew through me, numbing my fingers. Warming myself at the *kotatsu* electric foot warmer and talking to the owner of Nanbugama Craftsman, I was surprised to learn that he was a graduate of my art school and the go-between for our mutual friend, Makoto Nakamura. In addition, I met Kyubei Kiyomizu at a shooting location in Kyoto. He was the same old friend, Hiroshi Tsukamoto, who once helped me with my work soon after the War. I was able to meet him again by chance thirty years later. During my photographing expedition, I met people I never expected to see and had wonderful things happen to me. Heartwarming communications were cherished experiences particularly in this area. From a different aspect, it proved for me to be a great learning opportunity with a fruitful outcome.

As I was generally busy with my regular work on weekdays, I devoted Saturdays, Sundays, and holidays to shooting this collection. At times poor weather conditions such as heavy snow and rain impeded my progress. So, without knowing when I would be able to photograph, perseverance and patience were necessary.

For the last few years there have been suggestions to compile my work, and Mr Kuze, President of Graphic-sha Publishing Co, and the editorial staff vigorously encouraged me by extending their cooperation. As a result, I compiled the photographs taken up to now into one book narrowing it down to 400 houses and 471 photographs from a total of 600 houses and 10,000 photographs. I wanted some of it to contain works that could serve as reference material. The selection and layout caused me great anguish.

This is a "living study of *noren*" in the relationship of man to his environment, categorized according to my judgment to include appearance, trademark, and front entrance. Going beyond differences in climate and external appearances, I wanted the material that expressed the context of traditions and deep-rooted conservatism to focus attention on its cultural and traditional significance. I shall be glad if this one book of color photographs can prove of some use to people concerned with these issues.

東北

Tohoku District

1 Ota Family

1.2. Ota Family : The Ota Family, an old family of Tsunodate, is the proprietor of this kimono shop founded during the18th century. A simple *noren* with the store name inscribed with a single character hangs in the tradesman's house which was build with a deep interior and storage room. (Kakunodate)

3. Ando Brewery : This *miso* and soy sauce shop has been in business since the Edo Period. The *noren* hangs inside the entryway of the "Snow Country" style house built with a rear drawing room and a magnificent storage room. *Shiroiwayaki* bricks were used in the drawing room. (Kakunodate)

4. Saito Kisuke Hall : This hand-dye shop in Honjo which is a short distance from Akita has flourished since the Edo Period. This *noren* stored in the clay-walled storage room was saved from several large fires. Hung at each celebration, the gigantic 11-panel plant-dyed interior *noren* was dyed during the late 19th century and it is extraordinary that the colors are still vivid. The design resembles that of a Kaga *noren*. (Ugo Honjo)

5. Saito Kisuke Hall : The "Kamieshi" characters from long ago remain on the front exterior of the old tradesman's house, while the front *noren* simply has the shop name written on it.

2 Ota Family

3 Ando Brewery

4 Saito Kisuke Hall

5 Saito Kisuke Hall

6 Gozaku Morihisa

7 Suzuki Iron Cauldron Shop

8 Suzuki Iron Cauldron Shop

9 Watari Brewery

10 Watari Brewery

6. Gozaku Morihisa Store: This five-generation old general store has continued to flourish for over 150 years. It is known as Gozaku, a shortened name of Gozaku Kyubei. The number 9 is used as the emblem in this simple *noren*. (Morioka)
7. Suzuki Iron Cauldron Shop: This Nanbu iron cauldron shop has existed for sixteen generations since the 16th century and was patronized by the Nanbu feudal clan. The full-length *noren* is adorned with a brushstroke motif of an iron cauldron by Matsugoro Hirokawa. It is simple with a distinctive gusto. (Morioka)
8. Suzuki Iron Cauldron Shop: You can sense the presence of the master cauldron in the famous old Morioka house.
9. Watarai Brewery: The original was founded by Shinemon Tachibanaya (1615-24) and the Watarai family of Tomoe village opened a branch in 1857. The Watarai family is the present proprietor today of the *sake* brewery known for its *Dewa-no-Yuki* sake brand. This is the counting room *noren* at the Watarai Brewery's private records and file building. (Tsuruoka,Ohyama)
10. Watarai Brewery: This *noren* hangs in the storage room doorway of the files and records building.
11. Haneda Brewery: Founded in 1789 under the former name Omiya, it is renowned for its *sake* brand, *Shira-uma*. This is a room-divider *noren*. (Tsuruoka, Ohyama)

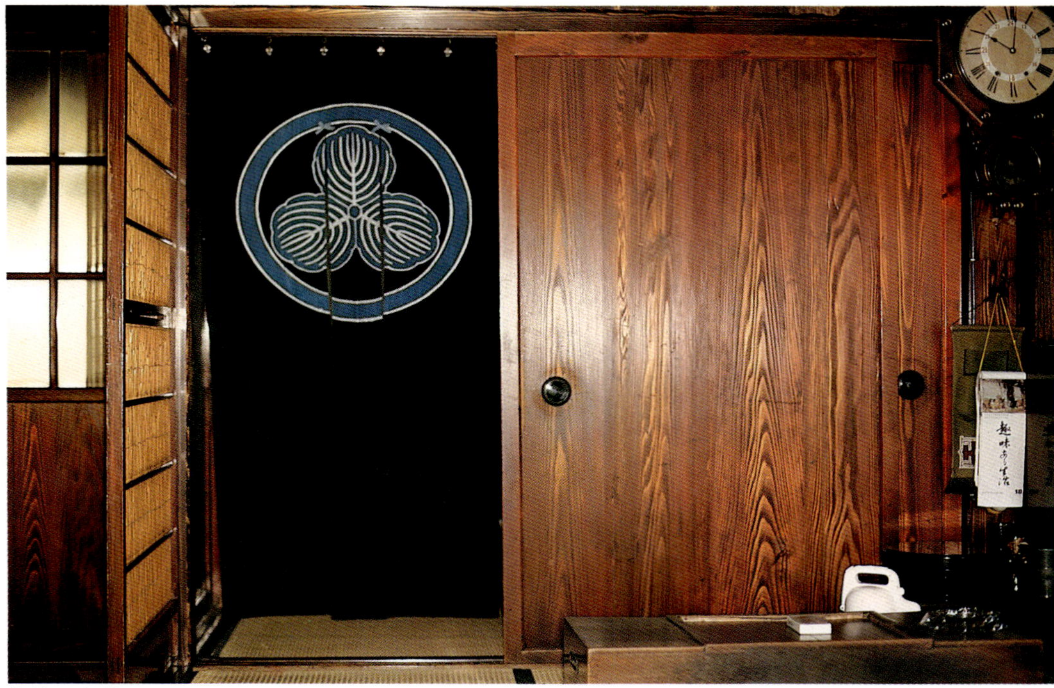
11 Haneda Brewery

12 Ishigura

13 Goto Used Furniture Store

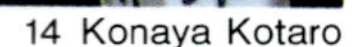
14 Konaya Kotaro

15 Ibishiya

16 Ishibashiya

12. Ishigura : This is an old, established footwear store long known for its handmade *geta* clogs. (Yonezawa)
13. Goto Used Furniture Store : The bric-a-brac beside the wooden lattice in front of the Tohoku used-furniture store adds an interesting touch. (Yonezawa)
14. Konaya Kotaro : A *noren* graces the entrance of a *kakekomi soba* buckwheat noodle shop that was patronized by the former Yonezawa feudal clan. (Yonezawa)
15. Ibishiya : The *noren* in the quiet and modest kimono shop is decorated with an elegant diamond-shaped motif. (Yonezawa)
16. Ishibashiya : This is a shop in Sendai near Miyazawa Bridge known for its handmade candy. The fringed edges of the *noren* harmonize splendidly with the tranquil exterior of the old house still in its original state. (Sendai)
17. Ishibashiya : The cord *noren* inside the store makes a pretty silhouette against the *shoji* door.

17 Ishibashiya

18 Aizu Aoi

21 Takefuji

19 Aizu Aoi

20 Suzukiya Rihei

18. Aizu Aoi: In olden Japan, Aizu Aoi was the store of the Aizu feudal clan. Today it is famous for its Aizu Aoi sweets. This *noren* which leads to the entrance of the storage room in the store is inscribed with the old Japanese character "Au" which was also the flag-insignia of the Aizu clan. (Aizu Wakamatsu)

19. Aizu Aoi: The white, five panel *noren* at the front entrance contrasts beautifully with the whitewashed walls and the intricate lattice woodwork.

20. Suzukiya Rihei: This store founded in 1830-44 sells lacquerware and other Japanese folkcrafts. The 150 year old house is built in the plaster storehouse style. The front entrance *noren* is rich in character conveying a sense of historical importance.(Aizu Wakamatsu)

21. Takefuji: Takefuji dating back to 1624 sells kitchenware and bamboo ware. Built with the typical Tohoku snow doors and earthen floor, traces of rope grooves can be seen on the tying post for cows. The parallel cross markings on the store's front *noren* looks beautiful when wet in a drizzle. (Aizu Wakamatsu)

22. Nagatoya: This is an old-fashioned candy shop established in 1848 that sells bird-and *daruma*-shaped candy. The faded *noren* of the old tradesman's house brings back fond memories. (Aizu Wakamatsu)

22 Nagatoya

23 Konohana Brewery

24 Mitsutaya

23. Konohana Brewery : Konohana Brewery has been a *sake* brewery over 300 years since the time of the historical figure Gamou. The *noren* with the white background makes an elegant contrast with the beautiful lattice of the tradesman's house. (Aizu Wakamatsu)

24. Mitsutaya : It has been known since ancient times for its homemade *Tenpo miso* and *miso dengaku*. The brushwork on the *noren* awning is interesting. (Aizu Wakamatsu)

25. 26. Tsuruizutsu : The building of this Aizu local cuisine restaurant belonged to a large landowner in Yama District (built in 1877). It was moved and remodeled leaving its original structure intact. The dark blue background of the *noren* blends in nicely with the rustic front exterior. (Aizu Wakamatsu)

27. Ebiya : This restaurant specializing in eel cuisine has over a hundred year old history in Aizu. The *noren* which has the single character "う" written on it and the inn-like *shoji* doors make an interesting combination. (Aizu Wakamatsu)

25 Tsuruizutsu

26 Tsuruizutsu

27 Ebiya

28 Takino

29 Narumiya

30 Naraya

28. Takino: This store is known for *wappa meshi*, a rice dish cooked in a bamboo steamer, from the remote area of Hinomata. (Aizu Wakamatsu)
29. Narumiya: The Japanese sweets shop founded in 1624 is famous for its *sake manju* cakes and *omameto* pea sweets. (Kitakata)
30. Naraya: Situated on the Shiokawa River not far from Aizu Wakamatsu, this Japanese sweets shop's elegant candy called *kokonoe* is popular today. We can catch a glimpse of the *noren* surviving through decades of wind and snow. (Aizu Shiokawa)

関東
Kanto District

1 Jusanya

2 Ohnoya

3 Yonoya

4 Domyo

5 Chikusen

1. Jusanya : Established in 1736, this shop has specialized in boxwood combs for fourteen generations. The name is derived from the Japanese word "kushi", meaning comb. A play on words, "ku" means nine and "shi" means four. Adding 9 and 4 gives the total of 13 which is "Jusan" in Japanese. The *noren* hanging in the store is ornamented with a bamboo leaf motif. (Tokyo)
2. Ohnoya : A six-generation old shop founded in 1772, Ohnoya is renowned for its dancing *tabi* footwear. Its building in Shintomi-cho has been standing since 1849. The subtle *noren* is very elegant. (Tokyo)
3. Yonoya : This comb shop in front of the Kannon Temple in Asakusa has been popular with the people around this temple for many generations. The *noren* in the shop is decorated with drawings of various combs. (Tokyo)
4. Domyo : Established in 1653, Domyo is a branch of Echigoya, the predecessor of Mitsukoshi. The eight-generation shop is located at Ikenohata in Ueno. The shop is known for its *kumihimo* braided cord and *obijime* sash band. The plum blossom on the *noren* represents the true essence of elegance. (Tokyo)
5. Chikusen : This is the *noren* of Chikusen, a store (1859) known since ancient times for its Edo *komon* fine-patterned crepe and Honzome *yukata* gown. (Tokyo)
6. Matsumoto : Matsumoto is a Kyoto style kimono shop in Nihonbashi. The large emblem of the pine tree on the awning *noren* is strikingly attractive. (Tokyo)

6 Matsumoto

7 Isetatsu

8 Isetatsu

7. Isetatsu : Isetatsu is a four generation old *chiyogami* figured paper store dating back to 1864. A simple, humble *noren* hangs over the front of the little store and built-in residence complex. Small figurines and other props complementing it produce "an enchanted wonderland" . (Tokyo)

8. Isetatsu : The *noren* inside the store is surrounded by *chiyogami* paper.

9. Kashiwaya : The *noren* of Kashiwaya, located in front of Yasukuni Shrine in Kanda, is long known for its *koto* and *sangen* musical instruments. (Tokyo)

10. 11. Hyotanya : These are the front and interior *noren* of the Asakusa Nakamise Store, an old store specializing in ivory works and *shamisen* attachments for four generation founded by a Tokugawa vassel at the end of the Meiji Restoration. (Tokyo)

12. Tsumugiya Kichibei : A seventh generation kimono shop with a 150 year old history, Tsumugiya Kichihei specializes in hand-wrung, hand-dyed, and hand-woven kimonos. The subtle *noren* and storefront present a graceful and refined setting in Ginza. (Tokyo)

13. 14. Fujiya : Fujiya is a specialty store in Asakusa renowned for the *tenugui* towels used in Japanese dances. The storefront *noren* is ornamented with wisteria flowers. The stylish *noren* in the store (left) is decorated with a print and solid background.(Tokyo)

9 Kashiwaya

10 Hyotanya

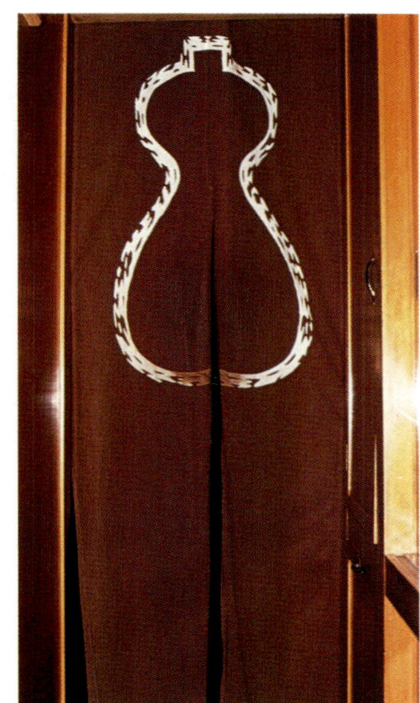
11 Hyotanya

12 Tsumugiya

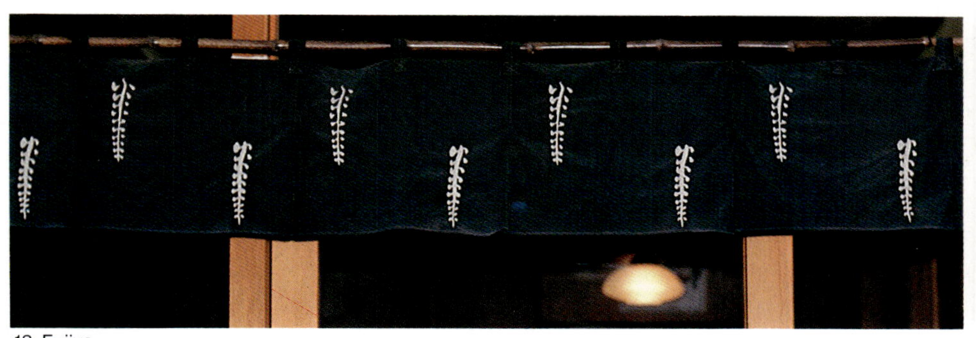
13 Fujiya

14 Fujiya

15 Ninben

16 Tamakiya

17 Kamishige

18 Ebiya

19 Tenyasu

15. Ninben : Established in 1699 and flourishing for twelve generations, Ninben is the oldest dried bonito shop. For generations the first character "I" of its original name, Iseya Ihei, was used on the *noren* and since then the shop has been called Ninben. (Tokyo)

16. Tamakiya : This *edomae tsukudani* shop has made savory delicacies simmered in soy sauce for seven generations since 1782. (Tokyo)

17. Kamishige : Kamishige is a *kamaboko* and *hanpen* fishmeat dumpling speciality store that has existed for six generations since 1688. (Tokyo)

18. Ebiya : This *edomae tsukudani* shop near Azuma Bridge has continued for four generations dating back to 1869. The *noren* in the store used a combination of symbols and characters in its designs. (Tokyo)

19. Tenyasu : Founded in Tsukudajima (1818-30), Tenyasu has been standing for 150 years as a Tsukudajima shop. The huge awning *noren* displayed in front of the small and quaint tradesman's house brings fond memories and nostalgia for old Japan. (Tokyo)

20 Osawa Tea Shop

20. Osawa Tea Shop: Going back five generations, this tea shop was founded in 1852 by Kakuzaemon Osawa, a tea inspector for the Shogun. This is the *noren* at the entrance to the kitchen of the Yushima shop. (Tokyo)

21. Shuetsu: The *fukujinzuke* relish shop originated with the founder Seiemon Noda in 1673-81 and received its name from Prince Mikado Atonomi a priest at the temple called Rinnoji. The illustrations on the *noren* are very intriguing. (Tokyo)

21 Shuetsu

22 Yamamoto Nori

22. Yamamoto Nori: This shop founded in 1849 has long been known for its *nori* seaweed. It is said that the Japanese plum blossom on the *noren* symbolizes the cold season when high grade seaweed is procured and the plum blossom bloom is at the height of its fragrance. (Tokyo)

23. Rengyoku-an: Rengyoku-an *soba* noodle shop founded by the Yasohachi Kubota in 1861 and has succeeded for six generations in Ikenohata. (Tokyo)

24. Yabusoba: Long ago Yabu was originally the Tsutaya shop at Dangozaka in Nezu. The *noren* was shared in the Meiji Period resulting in the Ikenohata branch. (Tokyo)

23 Rengyoku-an

24 Yabusoba

25 Izuei

26 Nakasei

27 Kaneda

28 Daikokuya

25. Izuei: This *unagi* eel restaurant has been serving eel dishes in Ikenohata for two hundred years, since 1772-81. (Tokyo)
26. Nakasei: This is the fourth generations Nakasei *tempura* restaurant. Founded in 1860, the shop was built in 1870 in front of Asakusa Kokaido Hall. (Tokyo)
27. Kaneda: This shop at Nakamise in Asakusa has been long known for its poultry dishes. (Tokyo)
28. Daikokuya: This is the *noren* at the front entrance of Daikokuya which has been popular among the Asakusa people for its Edo type *tempura*. This mallet symbol is eye-catching. (Tokyo)

29 Komagata Dojo

30 Iseki

31 Kuremutsu

29. Komagata Dojo : Founded in 1801, Komagata has continued for five generations. It was reconstructed after a large fire in 1806. The characters on the *noren* were written by Senkichi Shumokuya, one of the top sign painters in that era. (Tokyo)

30. Iseki : The three-generation old Iseki at Takabashi in Fukagawa was founded in 1868 and specializes in loach dishes. It still captures the old flavor of the "Edo Shitamachi" downtown atmosphere. (Tokyo)

31. Kuremutsu : A *sake* pub next to the Kannon Temple in Asakusa, Kuremutsu is an old-fashioned private house that was moved and renovated.
The decor includes much old, traditional Japanese furniture and other folk crafts. It is referred to as the "Ochiudo Teahouse" for casual visitors. The symbol on the *noren* makes an interesting contrast with the wooden mortar. (Tokyo)

32. Kuremutsu : This is the front exterior at twilight where the feeling of old *shitamachi* is effectively recaptured.

32 Kuremutsu

33 Goemon

34 Hisago

33. Goemon: Goemon is a restaurant at Hakusan in Hongo long known for its *tofu* dishes. The *noren* in the restaurant revives the number 5 of the Edo fireman's standard. (Tokyo)

34. Hisago: The Hisago *tofu* restaurant near Suehiro-tei in Shinjuku uses the gourd motif on the *noren* in the restaurant. (Tokyo)

35 Sasanoyuki

36 Nakae

37 Tomoegata

35. Sasanoyuki : This is the *noren* at the front entrance of Sasanoyuki which has specialized in *tofu* cuisine for over 270 years. Founded in 1703 by Chubei Tamaya who invented the soft *kinugoshi tofu*, the restaurant has continued for nine generations. (Tokyo)

36. Nakae : This is the *noren* at the front entrance of Nakae on the former Yoshiwara bank. It has been popular since ancient times for its *sakura nabe* casserole dish and other horse meat delicacies. (Tokyo)

37. Tomoegata : This is the *noren* in the *chanko ryori* restaurant in Ryogoku that was opened by the elderly ninth-generation *sumo* wrestler, Tomotsuna. Although the restaurant is new, the *noren* and decor skillfully captures the feeling of the *sumo* world. (Tokyo)

38. Edomasa : This is the *noren* at the front entrance of Edomasa located at the foot of Ryogoku Bridge. It is renowned for the *sumo* wrestler's patronage and its grilled eel. (Tokyo)

39. Uoju : Founded in 1688-1704, Uoju has been a long established caterer going back twelve generations. (Tokyo)

40. Michikusa : This is the front *noren* of a counter restaurant near the Asakusa Niōmon. The motif of strips of patterned ribbon makes an interesting design. (Tokyo)

38 Edomasa

39 Uoju

40 Michikusa

41 Habutae

42 Usagiya

43 Baikatei

44 Osakaya

41. Habutae: Established in 1819, Habutae was a teahouse in front of the Zensho Temple gate on the Oji Kaido Road. Later the present shop was rebuilt on Shimoya Imazaka. The six-generation old *dango* dumpling shop has been written about by the writers Soseki Natsume and Kyoka Izumi. (Tokyo)

42. Usagiya: The founder who was born in the year of the rabbit (*usagi*), gave the shop the name "usagi" in 1913. It is a Japanese sweets shop. (Tokyo)

43. Baikatei: The head shop, Shinkawa, was established in 1804-18 and known for its *taru senbei* crackers for six generations. This is the front *noren* of the *umemonaka*, the Fukagawa Nakamise shop. (Tokyo)

44. Osakaya: Osakaya has been making the *akiiro monaka* sweets for seventeen generations; it was founded in 1700. The brushwork on the sign was by Fusetsu Nakamura. (Tokyo)

45. Matsuzaki Senbei: Established in 1865, Matsuzaki Senbei changed its name from Mikawaya after the Kanto earthquake. It is a four-generation old *senbei* rice cracker shop. This is the recent *noren* of the shop. The teapot motif makes an exquisite design against the white background. (Tokyo)

46. Kototoi Dango: This five-generation old *dango* dumpling shop was established in 1869 and is located near Kototoi Bridge. (Tokyo)

47. Kyugetsu: This Japanese sweets shop is well known for its *agemanju* cakes by visitors to Fukagawa Fudo Shrine. (Tokyo)

48. Funabashiya: This *kuzu-mochi* rice cake shop was established in 1805 and has continued as a teahouse in front of the Kameido Tenjin Shrine gate for six generations. The calligraphy on the *noren* is by Eiji Yoshikawa. (Tokyo)

49. Chomeiji Sakura Mochi: The *sakura-mochi* rice cake shop was founded in 1717 and has existed for thirteen generations at Chomeiji Temple in Sumida. (Tokyo)

45 Matsuzaki Senbei

46 Kototoi Dango

47 Kyugetsu

48 Funabashiya

49 Chomeiji

50 Tachibana-ya

51 Iemotoya

52 Kiku-ya

53 Shimizu Kintsuba

50. Tachibana-ya : This is the front *noren* of the sixteenth-generation teahouse, Tachibanaya, located within the grounds of Toyokawa Inari Shrine on Aoyama Avenue. It is owned by the wife of the *Kabuki* actor, Uzaemon. The *Tachibana* flower in the store name is beautiful. (Tokyo)

51. Iemotoya : Existing since the Meiji Period, Iemotoya is also one of the teahouses at Toyokawa Inari Shrine. The front *noren* is adorned with a beautiful motif of the Yoshiwara chain. (Tokyo)

52. Kiku-ya : The motif of the Edo fireman's standard on the *noren* of the Kiku-ya teahouse within the same temple ground is beautiful. (Tokyo)

53. Shimizu Kintsuba : Shown here is the front *noren* of Shimizu Kintsuba, one of the teahouses at Fukagawa Fudo Shrine that is popular for its homemade *kintsuba* cakes. (Tokyo)

54. Amanoya : Founded in 1846, Amanoya has for five generations sold sweet *sake* near the *torii* at Kanda Myojin Shrine. It is also known for its *shibazaki natto* and *miso*. This is the *noren* leading into the kitchen. (Tokyo)

55. Enomotoen : This is the front entrance *noren* of an *arare* cracker shop in Ueno. This shop was originally established as a tea shop in the late Meiji era. (Tokyo)

56. Hanaya : This is the front *noren* of a sweets teahouse at Shimbashi known for its furnishings of a Kabuki stage. (Tokyo)

57. Mimasuya : The *noren* in the Japanese sweets shop, Mimasuya, on Aoyama Avenue. (Tokyo)

58. Sometaro : This is the *noren* in Sometaro, an *okonomi-yaki* Japanese pancake shop near Honganji Temple in Asakusa, which was used as a setting for Jun Takami's "Ikanaru Hoshi no Moto ni." (Tokyo)

54 Amanoya

55 Enomotoen

56 Hanaya

57 Mimatsuya

58 Sometaro

59 Kameya

60 Imoju

61 Miyaoka Machikan

59. Kameya: This is the *noren* over the front entrance of Kameya, a store built in the plaster storehouse style in Kawagoe City. It is close to 200 years old, dating back to 1783. It is known for *hatsukari-yaki*. (Kawagoe)

60. Imoju: Built in early Meiji, this shop is known for *imo senbei* crackers and other sweets made from sweet potatoes grown in Kawagoe. This is the *noren* over the front entrance. (Kawagoe)

61. Miyaoka Machikan: The front *noren* of a plaster storehouse style general store for kitchenware, etc. remains in its original state. (Kawagoe)

62. Sa-ami: This is an *unsui*, meatless cuisine restaurant near the Kamakura Hachiman Shrine. The powerful brushstrokes on the front *noren* go beautifully with the lush bamboo leaves and the white *shoji* doors. (Kamakura)

62 Sa-ami

北陸
Hokuriku District

1 Maruokaya

2 Takagi

3 Nakaya Druggist

1. Maruokaya: Clearly stating the services offered, the plain *noren* have hung at the entrance of the old rustic mill for generations. (Kanazawa)
2. Takagi: The macramé *noren* coordinates splendidly with the maltster built like an old tradesman's house with an old-fashioned stone slab lane. (Kanazawa)
3. Nakaya Druggist: This druggist, known for its *kongentan* herb preparation since early feudal days, has close to a 400-year-old history dealing in herb medicine. (Kanazawa)
4. Hayashiya Tea Shop: Founded in 1752, Hayashiya tea shop sells Uji tea. The *noren* decorated with a tea leaf and flower motif adds a tranquil touch to the over 200-year-old shop. (Kanazawa)
5. Fumuroya: Fumuroya, established in 1865, is a Kaga *fu* shop renowned for its *sudare-fu* dish, pieces of gluten bread covered with sweet and sour sauce, which is a specialty in Kaga. (Kanazawa)

4 Hayashiya Tea Shop

5 Fumuroya

6 Mochitomi

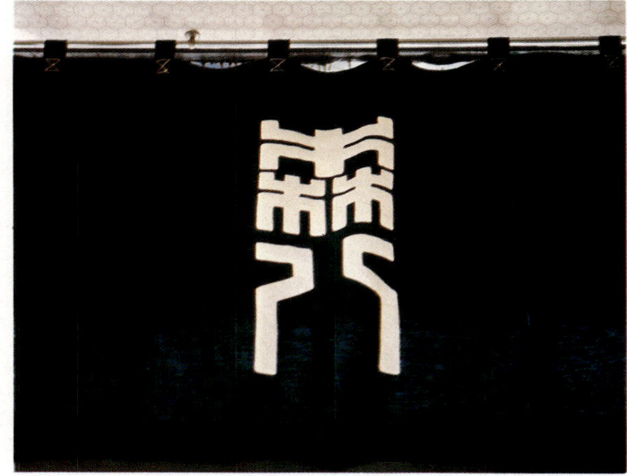

7 Morihachi

8 Morihachi

9 Moroeya

6. Mochitomi : This nostalgic *mochigashi* bean-jam cake shop is rich in local color. (Kanazawa)

7. 8. Morihachi, dating back to 1625, is a Japanese sweets shop famous for its *choseiden* cakes, a Kaga specialty. (Kanazawa)

9. Moroeya : Founded in 1849, Moroeya is a Kaga *rakugan* sweets shop. (Kanazawa)

10. Moroeya : The summer *noren* of Moroeya.

11. 12. Rakugan Bunko : The private Rakugan Exhibition Pavilion of Moroeya was an old tradesmen's house removed and reconstructed in another part of Kanazawa. (Kanazawa)

10 Moroeya

11 Rakugan Bunko

12 Rakugan Bunko

13 Tawaraya

13. Tawaraya : Tawaraya is a 150-year-old candy shop known for its hand-made candy. Although its *noren* has only characters printed on a heavy, white cotton cloth, it is nostalgic while at the same time crisp and striking. (Kanazawa)

14 Ohi-yaki Pottery

15 Tsuda Mizuhiki

16 Tochiori Dye Shop

17 Takezono Ornament Shop

18 Otomoro

14. Ohi-yaki Pottery : The reserved *noren* in front of Ohi-yaki pottery built similarly to a traditional *samurai* house sets an elegant and sonorous tone. (Kanazawa)
15. Tsuda Mizuhiki : An unusual *noren* made of twisted paper string decorates the window of the 150-year-old Tsuda Mizuhiki shop which makes the traditional Kaga two-tone paper cords for gift-wrapping. (Kanazawa)
16. Tochiori Dye Shop : This shop is known for its Kaga Yuzen silk. The persimmon-colored *noren* against the old wooden lattice background makes a fresh and attractive contrast. (Kanazawa)
17. Takezono Ornament Shop : This shop does gold-and silverwork and is well-known for gold leaf, a Kaga specialty. (Kanazawa)
18. Otomoro : Otomoro, founded during the late 17th to early 18th century, serves Kaga cuisine. (Kanazawa)
19. Goriya : The Gori cuisine of fresh-water fish is a Kanazawa specialty. (Kanazawa)
20. Jinbei : Jinbei, a branch of Tsubajin Inn which has a 270-year old history, specializes in Kaga cuisine. Shown here is the kitchen *noren* of Jinbei. The design with the sword guard motif is simple and at the same time beautiful. (Kanazawa)

19 Goriya

20 Jinbei

21 Kita-Shuzo Brewery

22 Kita-Shuzo Brewery

23 Kita-Shuzo Brewery

24 The Kaga *noren* of the Kita Family

21. Kita-Shuzo Brewery : Kita Shuzo is renowned for brewing *shojo*, a local *sake* brand of Kaga. The *noren* stamped with the *shojo* brand name hangs at the entrance of the memorial hall. (Nonoichi)

22. Kita-Shuzo Brewery : The external appearance of the entrance resembles that of a typical shop during the feudal era.

23. Kita-Shuzo Brewery : This Kaga *noren*, which was used in everyday living, acted as a room divider and screen. The simple repeated curved line design is just as graceful and refreshing today.

24. The Kaga *noren* of the Kita Family : It was a Kaga custom that the *noren* was part of the bridal trousseau. The family crest was located at the top center, while auspicious motifs decorated the bottom. After a few days following the wedding, the *noren* could be seen hanging in the wedding couple's parlour. Today, this custom is still practiced in some parts of Kuchinoto district. Although most are made of silk, the *chirimen* crepe of Kaga Yuzen silk is very gorgeous. (Nonoichi)

25 Tatsuno Tatami Shop

26 Moroeya

27 Hirasawa Family

28 Hirasawa Family

25. Tatsuno Tatami Shop: This Kaga *noren* was used by the Tatsuno family. The white print on the cotton background is very vivid and lovely. (Kanazawa)

26. Moroeya: This Kaga *noren* was used at the shop counter of the Kaga *rakugan* sweets shop, Moroeya. (Kanazawa)

27. 28. Hirasawa Family: This bridal *noren* graced the Hiraju tea utensil shop. (Kanazawa)

29 Nakamiya Family

30 Nakamiya Family

31 Ogawa Family

29. 30. Nakamiya Family: These *noren* were part of the bridal trousseau of the Nakamiya family, proprietors of the Morihachi shop famous for their Kaga sweets called *choseiden*. (Kanazawa)

31. 32. Ogawa Family: These bridal Kaga *noren* belonged to the Ogawa family who dealt with Kaga Yuzen silk. (Kanazawa)

32 Ogawa Family

33 Ikedaya

34 Daimonya

35 Daimonya

33. Ikedaya : Ikedaya was an herb medicine shop founded in 1830. The *hangontan noren* brings back fond memories of old-fashioned drug stores. (Toyama)
34. Daimonya : This kimono shop known for its Hakusan *tsumugi* fabric was established in 1818. Hung in the shop's sitting room, this *noren* was cotton dyed with plant dye. (Echizen Ohno)
35. Daimonya : The double *noren* of the rear entrance.

中部
Chubu District

1 Yomogiya

2 Kikyoya

3 Tajimaya

1. Yomogiya: Toson Shimazaki's son manages the folkcrafts section at Yomogiya Inn. The old *noren* and lantern impart the atmosphere of Kisoji Road. (Magome)
2. Kikyoya: The building dates back to the Edo period. The main thoroughfare name, Nakasen-do, written on the *shoji* screen and the single character at the top right-hand corner of the *noren* also reflects the quaintness of the old inn. (Magome)
3. Tajimaya: A simple *noren* hanging from the eave and an old-fashioned straw raincoat and hat at the door typify a tavern on Kisoji Road. (Magome)
4. Daikokuya: This is a full-length room-dividing *noren* at Daikokuya, a folkcraft shop. In the past it was the home of Toson Shimazaki's first love, Oyu and the first liquor shop on Kisoji Road. (Magome)
5. Daikokuya: The *noren* hangs from the eaves of the front exterior.
6. Shinya: This is the full-length *noren* at the entrance of Shinya known for its *goheimochi* rice cakes, a Kiso specialty. (Tsumago)

4 Daikokuya

5 Daikokuya

6 Shinya

7 Koshinzuka

7. Koshinzuka : This is an old inn situated on a mountain ridge. The simple markings on the faded bamboo *noren* go well with the bamboo basket and gourd containers hanging from the eaves. (Tsumago)

8. Yamagiri : The *noren* stretches under the eaves across the front exterior. It conjures up the delicious aroma of Japanese boiled vegetables, even to the sign on the *shoji* doors. (Tsumago)

9. Tsuchiya : A faded *noren* hangs under the eaves. The characters written on the *shoji* door convey the mood of the old relay station.(Tsumago)

10. Manjuya : Manjuya has been famous for its Oriku combs since the 18th century. (Yabuhara)

11. Tokkuriya : A half-length *noren* hangs over the doorway of the former old inn. Today the inn has been converted into a historical museum. (Narai)

12. Tsuchiya : The *noren* strung under the eaves across the front exterior along with the wooden lattice and *shoji* doors casts a tranquil mood over the teahouse. (Narai)

8 Yamagiri

9 Tsuchiya

10 Manjuya

11 Tokkuriya

12 Tsuchiya

13 Hidaminzoku-Kokokan

13. Hidaminzoku-Kokokan : This was the house of a doctor during the 18th century. The swirl of the *magatama*, comma-shaped beads, forms an intriguing motif on the *noren*. (Takayama)
14. Yoshijima Family: The double bar motif on the full-length *noren* at the entrance is said to have been bestowed by the shogunate government upon paying taxes. (Takayama)
15. Kusakabe Family : Preserving its original form, this is the oldest house in Takayama built during the 19th century. A full-length *noren* hangs at the doorway. (Takayama)
16. Hisadaya : This is the full-length *noren* of an inn with a 180-year-old history that was formerly a *manju* cake shop. (Takayama)
17. Sakaguchiya : Sakaguchiya was built in the late 19th century in the style of a tradesman's house. The inn's full-length *noren* evokes the mood of Hida Road. (Takayama)
18. Sumiyoshi : This *noren* conceals a storage room built in the house next to the entrance of an old inn. The lines of the swirl curve gracefully. (Takayama)

14 Yoshijima

15 Kusakabe Family

16 Hisadaya

17 Sakaguchiya

18 Sumiyoshi

19 Uchihoya

20 Uchihoya

21 Uchihoya

19. Uchihoya: This shop, established in 1769, sells candles and hair oil. The long *noren* curtaining the entire front exterior has an impressive impact. (Takayama)
20. Uchihoya: On the interior, the *noren* emblem is linked to form a chain.
21. Uchihoya: A linen *noren* hangs inside the entrance.
22. Uchihoya: A large 7-panel interior *noren* is used as a room divider in the drawing room.

22 Uchihoya

23 Ohnoya

24 Tajikaya

23. Ohnoya : The *noren* at the doorway of the teahouse goes beautifully with the unique style of lattice found in this district. (Takayama)

24. Tajikaya : The *noren*, *shoji* doors, and old inn lantern provide the teahouse with the atmosphere of an old-fashioned relay station. (Takayama)

25. Baren : This is a woodblock print tea-shop. The *baren* used in woodblock printing provides an interesting motif in the *noren*. (Takayama)

26. Karako : The old Sakaguchiya inn is the proprietor of this Japanese sweets teahouse. The cool color of the *noren* and the white *shoji* door makes a fresh, striking contrast. (Takayama)

27. Notoya : This Japanese sweets tea-house is known for *warabi mochi* and powdered green tea used in the tea ceremony. The atmosphere of this area is reflected in this shop. (Takayama)

25 Baren

26 Karako

27 Notoya

28 Niki Brewery

28. Niki Brewery : Niki Brewery, known for the local brand, *Tamanoi*, has been making *sake* since 1695. A dark, rich brown *noren* hangs over the entrance of the brewery which is built like a typical Takayama house.(Takayama)
29. Ohnoya : Ohnoya makes Takayama *miso*. The kitchen *noren* surrounded by barrels of *miso* is printed with the Takeda lozenge emblem.(Takayama)
30. Funasaka Brewery : This brewery makes the local brand, *Miyamagiku*.
31. Oida Brewery : This brewery makes the local brands, *Onikoroshi* and *Hida Jiman*.
32. Kawajiri Brewery : This brewery makes the local brand, *Hida Masamune*.
33. Hirase Brewery : This brewery makes the local brand, *Kusudama*.
34. Harada Brewery : This brewery makes the local brand, *Dashi*.
(Takayama)

29 Ohnoya

30 Funasaka Brewery

31 Oida Brewery

32 Kawajiri Brewery

33 Hirase Brewery

34 Harada Brewery

35 Susaki

37 Kadomasa

36 Kotoriya

35. Susaki: The architecture and the savory taste of the cuisine (*sowa*-style *honzen kuzushi*) fully captures the local color of Takayama. (Takayama)

36. Kotoriya: Kotoriya is a kimono shop in Kami-Sannomachi. The first character of the proprietor's name is used on the *noren* at the front entrance. (Takayama)

37. Kadomasa: This restaurant is renowned for its traditional Takayama *shojin* cuisine and refined formalities. (Takayama)

38 Shiramasa

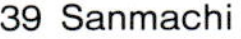

39 Sanmachi

40 Chotakubo-Ichimi- Itto Carvings

41 Watanabe Seikodo

38. Shiramasa: The oldest shop in Takayama deals with antique art. The writing style on the linen *noren* is unique and has a distinct character. (Takayama)
39. Sanmachi: This folk-arts and -craft shop is known for Hida-Sashiko quilting. (Takayama)
40. Chotakubo-Ichimi-Itto Carvings: This shop is noted for wood carvings of Japanese yew, a Hida specialty. (Takayama)
41. Watanabe Seikodo: A simple *noren* with only the characters written on it hangs under the eaves of a paper-hanger shop's front exterior. (Takayama)
42. Nakanoya: The motif on the *noren* of Nakanoya, a folkcraft souvenir shop, is fresh and crisp. (Takayama)

42 Nakanoya

43 Matsumoto-Mingeikan

44 Omodakaya

45 Sakuramamiya

46 Watanabe Dyers

43. Matsumoto-Mingeikan: This is the private folkcraft museum of Taro Maruyama, an ethnographic researcher. The *noren* of the house appears in its original state. (Matsumoto)
44. Omodakaya: An old house in Gujo Hachiman, the souvenir shop is also a folklore museum. (Gujo Hachiman)
45. Sakuramamiya: A large awning *noren* hangs over the entrance of Sakuramamiya which is famous for its cinnamon candy, a local specialty. (Gujo Hachiman)
46. Watanabe Dyers: The building is constructed like an old-fashioned tradesman's house with thick lattice. In the local area the dye shop is called Konya. (Gujo Hachiman)
47. Tsuboi Flag and Streamer Shop: This shop specializes in dyeing flags, streamers, screens and so on. The kite with a *samurai* face is impressive against the white background. (Gujo Hachiman)
48. Tsuboi Streamer Shop: A *noren* of *samurai* prints hangs in the entrance.

47 Tsuboi Flag and Streamer Shop

48 Tsuboi Streamer Shop

49 Oiwake-Yokan

50 Oiwake-Yokan

51 Yamadaichi

52 Sekibeya

53 Chojiya

49. Oiwake-Yokan: This is the awning *noren* of Oiwake-Yokan which has been known for its Oiwake-Yokan jelly since the 19th century. The shop is located near Shimizu Port. (Shimizu)
50. Oiwake-Yokan: The front exterior is rich with character, while the wording on the awning *noren* is interesting.
51. Yamadaichi: This full-length *noren* hangs in an *abekawa mochi* shop which was renovated from an old house near the Toro ruins. (Shizuoka)
52. Sekibeya: Sekibeya appeared in the "Fifty-three Stages of the Tokaido" and is also an *abekawa mochi* shop. (Shizuoka)
53. Chojiya: This *tororo* soup shop is the former Maruko Inn illustrated in Hiroshige's "Fifty-three Stages of the Tokaido." The *shoji* doors, wooden bench, oil-paper umbrella, cart and other objects bring fond memories of the old relay station during the 19th century. The lantern and *noren* also evoke the past. (Shizuoka Maruko)
54. Taigetsu: The *tororo* soup restaurant near Togetsuho in Shizuoka sets a tranquil scene. (Shizuoka Maruko)
55. Kaisaku: Kaisaku serves a shellfish cuisine in Shizuoka City, and has been in business for fifty years. A repeated motif of the store name is displayed on the *noren*. (Shizuoka)

54 Taigetsu

55 Kaisaku

56 Okakane Shop

57 Tokugetsu

58 Myokoen

56. Okakane Shop : Near Narumi Inn on the Tokaido Road, the Okakane Shop in Arimatsu specializes in white-spotted cotton fabrics called Arimatsu *shibori*. The Arimatsu *shibori noren* hanging in the entrance is unique. (Arimatsu)
57. Tokugetsu : Established in 1828, long ago, Tokugetsu was a distinguished restaurant. It has now become a Japanese pickle shop noted for its Moriguchi pickles. A simple motif of a moon which is taken from the Tokugetsu name adorns the *noren*. The Japanese characters are said to have been written by the Ukiyoe artist, Koka Yamamura. (Nagoya)
58. Myokoen : This is the *noren* leading to the kitchen of Myokoen. Myokoen was established at the beginning of the 20th century. Both making and selling green tea are its specialties.(Nagoya)

59 Kawabun

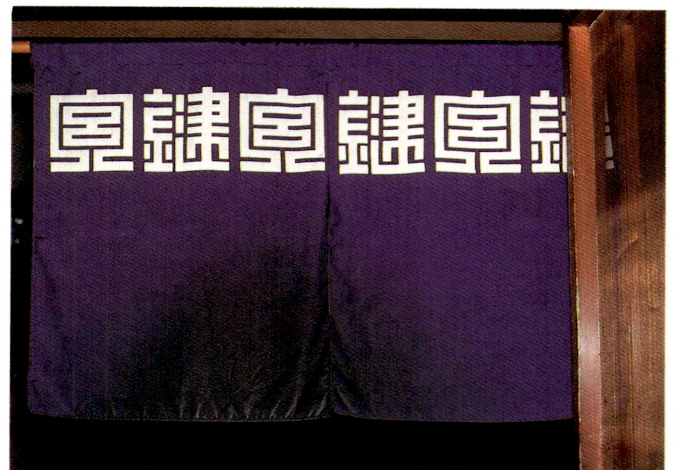

60 Miyaken

61 Ryoguchiya Korekiyo

62 Minochu

63 Suzume-Odori Sohonke

59. Kawabun : This inn in Marunouchi near the Nagoya Castle has existed from the 18th century. The *noren* leading to the kitchen is designed with the inn's name written as one large character. (Nagoya)
60. Miyaken : Miyaken is an old Japanese restaurant near Yanagibashi that is renowned for its poultry dishes. The store name is repeated across the *noren* leading to the kitchen. (Nagoya)
61. Ryoguchiya Korekiyo : A sweets shop established in 1634 and patronized by the former Owari feudal clan, it is known for *futari-shizuka* cakes. The *noren* with the white background displays the personality of the shop. (Nagoya)
62. Minochu : Minochu was founded in 1854 and is an old one-story house with a roof of Mikawa tiles near Gojobashi Bridge. Existing for five generations, it is noted for its *agari-yokan* jelly. (Nagoya)
63. Suzume-Odori Sohonke : Suzume-Odori Sohonke is a five generation-old Japanese sweets shop founded during 1854-60. A motif of the Suzume-Odori dance decorates the *noren* leading to the kitchen. (Nagoya)

64 Aoyagi Sohonke

64. 65. Aoyagi Sohonke: Shown here are the front *noren* (top) and the kitchen *noren* (bottom) of the one hundred year old Aoyagi Sohonke (1879) which is famous for *uiro* sweet rice jelly. The motif of a frog jumping in a circle of willow leaves is interesting. (Nagoya)

66. Akafuku Honpo: Founded in 1707, this shop is known for *akafuku mochi*, a specialty of Ise. The venerable age of Akafuku Honpo can be felt in the gabled-entrance of the old merchant's house, the huge carved store sign and the tea shop like *noren*. (Ise)

65 Aoyagi Sohonke

66 Akafuku Honpo

近畿

Kinki District

1 Raku Kichizaemon Pottery

2 Kiyomizu Rokubei Pottery

1. Raku Kichizaemon Pottery : This old house has a 400-year-old history, and it has been fourteen generations since the founder, Chojiro, began making Rakuyaki pottery (1573-92) under the guidance of Sen-no-Rikyu. It is said that during the second Kichizaemon generation the designation of "Tenka-Ichi" and the gold seal of "Raku" was bestowed by Hideyoshi. The white *noren* hanging in the entrance reminds us of the history and events behind it. (Kyoto)
2. Kiyomizu Rokubei Pottery: Since ancient times Gojozaka slope from Gojozaka Bridge to Higashi Oji was the gathering place of Kiyomizu potters. The first kiln was said to be initiated two hundred years ago. The brushwork of Ruisei Toshi on the front *noren* of the fifth generation of potters is magnificent. (Kyoto)
3. Miyawaki Baisen'an : This is a five-generation-old shop founded in 1823 that specializes in Kyoto fans. The contrast of *noren* and fans goes elegantly with the *mushiko* windows and old-fashioned bench of the old tradesman's house. (Kyoto)

4. 5. Ippodo Tea Shop : This Uji tea shop was founded in 1846 and has existed for five generations. The old tradesman's house is in its original state. The winter *noren* (left) and the summer *noren* (right) remind one of an Edo merchant's house. (Kyoto)

3 Miyawaki Baisen'an

4 Ippodo Tea Shop

5 Ippodo Tea Shop

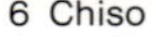

6 Chiso

7 Yashirojin

8 Yamaguchigen

6. Chiso: This Kyoto kimono (Yuzen) shop was established in 1604. The *chigiri-banamon* motif on the dark blue *noren* hanging over the front entrance is distinguished by its age as it pleasantly greets the eye. (Kyoto)
7. Yashirojin: This Kyoto kimono shop dates back to 1720. The shop name, Kondaya, graces the *noren* leading to the living quarters. (Kyoto)
8. Yamaguchigen: Founded in 1873, the old name of the Kyoto kimono shop is inscribed on the *noren* that leads to the living quarters. (Kyoto)
9. Chikiriya: Chikiriya was founded in 1725 and given its name by the founder, Yohei Nagano. However, this Kyoto kimono shop became known by the *hagoromo*, feathered-robe, trademark. The white *noren* in the entrance coordinates splendidly with the architecture of the building. (Kyoto)
10. Okakei: In 1586 Hanbei Nakamura established the fabric shop, Kariganeya. This shop was succeeded by Keizo Okamoto, founder of Okakei, in 1919. The *karigane* emblem of wild geese on the *noren* is exquisite. (Kyoto)

9 Chikiriya

10 Okakei

11 Sasau

12 Sasau

13 Higoya

11. Sasau: Sasau is an eight-generation-old Kyoto kimono shop dating back to 1738. This priceless *noren* was displayed at the Japanese Folkcraft Pavillion at the 1970 International Exposition. (Kyoto)
12. Sasau: This front entrance *noren* was made in 1868. Although frayed with age, the bold bamboo leaves are still resplendent.
13. Higoya: This is the *noren* at the front entrance of a dyeing and weaving shop in Nishijin. (Kyoto)
14. Senshoku Shop: This *noren* hangs over the entrance of the Senshoku shop, a dyeing and weaving shop in Nishijin. The design of a triangle is simple and elegant. (Kyoto)
15. Iwata: This *noren* hangs in a Kyoto kimono shop known particularly for its *obi* sashes in Sanjo at Karasuma Avenue. (Kyoto)
16. Ishikawa: This is a *noren* at the front entrance of a Kyoto kimono shop in Anekoji on Sakaimachi Street. (Kyoto)
17. Izukura: This *noren* leads to the living quarters of the Izukura Kyoto kimono shop famous for its Izukura *obi* sashes. (Kyoto)
18. Noguchi: This eight-generation-old Kyoto kimono shop dates back to 1734. The founder, Yasubei Kaneya, opened the shop under the name of Kaneyasu during the reign of the shogunate Yoshimune Tokugawa. (Kyoto)

14 Senshoku Shop

15 Iwata

16 Ishikawa

17 Izukura

18 Noguchi

19 Obiya Sutematsu

20 Obiya Sutematsu

21 Utsugi

22 Yamasho

19. Obiya Sutematsu: This Nishijin *obi* sash shop dates back to the 18th century. The simple *noren* beautifully complements the red-ochre lattice and *mushiko* windows which are typical features of a Nishijin style town-house. (Kyoto)
20. Obiya Sutematsu: This *noren* with a white background is hung for the New Year.
21. Utsugi: This Nishijin fabric shop is located in Ohmiya on Nakasuji Street. The large *noren* employs characters for its emblem. (Kyoto)
22. Yamasho: Yamasho is located in Ohmiya Higashi on Kamitachiuri Street. This Nishijin weaver has been known since ancient times for its hand-woven fabrics. The *noren* with a white background sets a lovely scene against the old tradesman's house. (Kyoto)
23. Tatsumi: This *noren* leads to the living quarters of a Nishijin weaver. (Kyoto)
24. Kano: This *noren* leads to the living quarters of a Nishijin weaver. (Kyoto)
25. Daisho: This *noren* leads to the living quarters of a Nishijin weaver. (Kyoto)

23 Tatsumi

24 Kano

25 Daisho

27 Sumiya

27. Sumiya: Originally established in 1589, the location was moved and the present restautrant was constructed at Ageya-cho in Shimabara in 1640. Long ago it was a popular brothel area famous for the beautiful woman, Yoshino Dayu. Today, it is a Japanese restaurant with a thirteen-generation history. The building was remodeled during the period of 1718-89 and left almost in its original state. It is said to be the only such house left. One can sense the long history behind this fascinating *noren*. (Kyoto)

28 Wachigaiya

29 Ichiriki

30 Fumiyo

28. 31. Wachigaiya: Wachigaiya, a brothel long ago in Shimabara, is now a Japanese restaurant. The building was constructed in 1856. The *noren* with the interlinking circles hangs inside the entrance (left), while the *noren* on the right is a room divider. (Kyoto)

29. Ichiriki: The walls of Ichiriki Japanese restaurant, established during 1688-1704, are a sober red ochre. Located on the south side of Gion-machi, this restaurant has a 300-year old history extending over twelve generations. (Kyoto)

30. Fumiyo: The Japanese restaurant of Fumiyo has continued for eight generations dating back to 1804-18. The *noren* dyed with the gentle, single character "富" is lovely. One can sense the influence of the succeeding generations of women proprietors as well as the city of Kyoto. (Kyoto)

31 Wachigaiya

32 Nakazato

33 Nakazato

34 Nakahata

35 Omasa

36 Hiiragiya

32. Nakazato : Located in Kami Shichiken near Kitano Shrine, this old Japanese restaurant dates back to the 19th century. The brownish orange front *noren* looks refreshing with the traditional beauty of the old Kyoto house enhanced by the wooden lattice and *mushiko* windows. (Kyoto)
33. Nakazato : This *noren* hangs inside the entrance.
34. Nakahata : This old Japanese restaurant is located near Gion Shinbashi. The bamboo front exterior and the *noren* behind the lattice make an intriguing combination. (Kyoto)
35. Omasa : This restaurant is located on the Yamato Oji Road in Gion. The character "大" in the store name is elegantly connected in two rows in front *noren*. (Kyoto)
36. Hiiragiya : This is the *noren* leading to the kitchen of an old inn founded in 1861. The character "Hiiragi," holly, used in the store name declares a deep faith in the Hiiragi Shrine (Holly) in Shimokamo. (Kyoto)
37. Tawaraya : This is the *noren* leading to the kitchen of Tawaraya, an old inn with a 250-year-old history traced back to 1704-11. The single character written in black ink against the white linen background is bold and decisive. (Kyoto)
38. Osawa : Osawa is a Gion restaurant across the Shirakawa River near the monument inscribed with a short poem written by Isamu Yoshii. The single plum blossom daintily adorns the *noren*.(Kyoto)

37 Tawaraya

38 Osawa

40 Nakamuraro Niken Teahouse

41 Nakamuraro Niken Teahouse

42 Yamabana Heihachi

43 Hiranoya

40. 41. Nakamuraro Niken Teahouse: As there were two teahouses inside the gate of Yasaka Shrine from ancient times, Nakamuraro Niken derived its name as the second teahouse. With a 400-year old history, it is popular for its *dengaku* boxed lunch and *Kaiseki* Kyoto-style cuisine. (Kyoto)

42. Yamabana Heihachi: Yamabana Heihachi, which is a restaurant specializing in freshwater fish, faces the Takano River in Yamabana. Built during the 17th century, the nineteen-generation-old front exterior brings back fond memories of the past. (Kyoto)

43. Hiranoya: Dating from the early 17th century, Hiranoya has a four hundred year history of *ayu*, sweetfish, cuisine. It is located in Kiyotaki in Arashiyama. (Kyoto)

44. Tsutaya: Tsutaya is also an *ayu* sweetfish restaurant at the same location as Hiranoya with the same length of history. Both are popular with worshipers at Atago Shrine. This photo was taken ten years ago when the thatched roof was in poor condition.

45. Tsutaya: This is the present appearance of Tsutaya after a portion was remodeled. The double eaves, which are typical features of teahouses, and the *noren* go beautifully together.

44 Tsutaya

45 Tsutaya

46 Shimokamo Teahouse

46. Shimokamo Teahouse: Shimokamo Teahouse, founded on the bank of Kamogawa River in 1856, serves Kyoto-style cuisine and is famous for its *hanami* boxed lunch. Although the building bas been reconstructed, the front exterior still retains the appearance of an old-fashioned teahouse. (Kyoto)

47 Shorankyo

48 Minokichi

49 Doraku

50 Kifuji

51 Mankamero

47. Shorankyo: Shorankyo is a restaurant and Japanese inn in Arashiyama known for its *kaede* boxed lunch. The motif of the character "居" encircled by a pine tree is simple and beautiful. (Kyoto)

48. Minokichi: Founded during 1716-36, this Kyoto-style restaurant is renowned for freshwater fish dishes and *seiro* boxed lunch. (Kyoto)

49. Doraku: This Kyoto cuisine restaurant has over a 350 year history dating back to around 1624-44. The *noren* made of small gourds strung together recreates the atmosphere of a restaurant in a temple town. (Kyoto)

50. Kifuji: Built near the Jurakudai ruins of Hideyoshi's castle, Kifuji is known for its first-class cuisine. The gourd motif on the *noren* goes splendidly with the red walls. (Kyoto)

51. Mankamero: Mankamero was founded in Nishijin during 1716-36 and has been known since ancient times for its first-class cuisine. The front *noren* of the twenty-ninth generation of the main Ikuma school displays a kind of purity in the lines. (Kyoto)

52. Minoko: This *kaiseki* restaurant is located in front of the south gate of Yasaka Shrine. There is a refined elegance in the faded *noren*. (Kyoto)

53. Tamanoya: Tamanoya is in front of the *torii* gate of Yasaka Shrine. The single character against the white background is refined and elegant. (Kyoto)

52 Minoko

53 Tamanoya

54 Ikkyu

54. Ikkyu: Founded around 1469-87, this *shojin* restaurant goes back almost five hundred years and twenty-six generations. It is located in front of the Daitokuji Temple. A simple *noren* hangs gracefully over the quiet and peaceful entrance. (Kyoto)

55 Tsujitome

56 Kakiden

57 Kikunoi

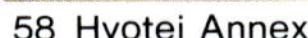

58 Hyotei Annex

59 Hyotei Annex

55. Tsujitome: This *kaiseki* restaurant lies east of the Sanjo Ohashi Bridge. The white *noren* hangs inside the entrance of the subdued and humble townhouse. (Kyoto)

56. Kakiden: Kakiden was founded in 1720 going back 250 years and nine generations. It serves *kaiseki* for tea and is also a caterer. Built like an ordinary tradesman's house, the trademark is conservative and unassuming. (Kyoto)

57. Kikuno: Kikuno also has a Kyoto-style restaurant in Makuzugahara in Maruyama. (Kyoto)

58. 59. Hyotei Annex: Hyotei Annex was founded in 1837 and is near Nanzenji. It is the annex of Hyotei that has specialized in *kaiseki* cuisine for fourteen generations. It is known for its *asagayu* dish in the summer and *uzuragayu* dish in the winter. The gourds on the front *noren* are superb in design. (Kyoto)

60. Hiranoya: Founded around 1716-36, it lies in Maruyama Park. Specializing in *imobo* cuisine, the restaurant has been handed down from one generation to another for three hundred years. The long *noren* with the white background hanging in front of the entrance vividly portrays its character. (Kyoto)

60 Hiranoya

61 Toriyasa

62 Toriyasa

63 Torishin

61. Toriyasa: This restaurant, which serves poultry and *mizutaki*, has close to a 200-year history that can be traced back to 1788. The outer *noren* and the long inner *noren* make an interesting contrast. (Kyoto)

62. Toriyasa: The old tradesman's house in Kiya-machi on Shijo-Avenue has a wide entrance and dates back to the late 19th century. The rich brown *noren* harmonizes tastefully with the black lattice. (Kyoto)

63. Torishin: Located near Shirakawa in Gion, it has long been known for its poultry dishes. (Kyoto)

64. Daichi: The close to 300-year old Daichi specializes in mud-turtle dishes. It is located in Goban-cho where vestiges of the old brothels remain. The short *noren*, with the name Daichi outlined, stretching across the front entrance is beautiful. The *noren* and the architecture of the building reminds us of the late 18th century style in old Edo. (Kyoto)

65. Warajiya: The 400-year-old Warajiya, which is located near the temple, Sanjusangendo, at the starting point of the former Yamato Road, introduced eel rice porridge. The restaurant's name is said to be derived from the story of Hideyoshi removing straw sandals (*waraji*) and putting them inside his clothes to warm them for his commander, Nobunaga. (Kyoto)

66. Juichiya: Juichiya originated as a teahouse at the starting point of Wakasa Road in Yamabana. Presently, it is a restaurant specializing in catfish and carp dishes. The building dates to the mid-19th century. (Kyoto)

64 Daichi

65 Warajiya

66 Juichiya

67 Nakamura

68 Yoshikawa

69 Shiruko

67. Nakamura : Nakamura serves Kyoto-style cuisine. The calm and subdued exterior of the building makes an interesting contrast with the *noren* at the front entrance and the bamboo fence. (Kyoto)

68. Yoshikawa : Yoshikawa is a *tempura* restaurant on Tominokoji Road. The short *noren* at the front entrance is simple and lovely with its white emblem. (Kyoto)

69. Shiruko : Shiruko is long established caterer known for Rikyu boxed lunch and soups. The large character "汁" on the white *noren* makes an impressive front entrance. (Kyoto)

70. Junidanya : Located near Gion Ichiriki, Junidanya is known for *kyochazuke* and *tempura*. Although the building is new, the architecture fully captures the flavor of Kyoto folkcraft. The comma-shaped heraldic design in the front *noren* is vivid and fresh. (Kyoto)

71. Izuu : Founded around 1781-89, Izuu is situated in the middle of Gion-machi and noted for its mackerel *sushi*. Shown here is a half-length *noren* in the restaurant. (Kyoto)

72. Yuranosuke : Located near Gion Ichiriki, Yuranosuke serves Kyoto cuisine and *kama-meshi* rice. The restaurant proprietor who liked Yuranosuke gave the restaurant this name. The comma-shaped design on the *noren* is refined and elegant. (Kyoto)

73. Takasebune : Takasebune is a pub near Kiyamachi that serves appetizers and *tempura*. The bamboo leaves are drawn in white on the dark blue *noren*. (Kyoto)

74. Mutsumi : This Kyoto-style restaurant in front of Yasaka Shrine's *torii* is famous for its *horakuyaki*. The white *kuyo* motif of nine circles appears resplendently on the front *noren*. (Kyoto)

70 Junidanya

71 Izuu

72 Yuranosuke

73 Takasebune

74 Mutsumi

75 Kawamichiyamisoka'an

76 Gonbei

77 Owariya

78 Chagetsu

75. Kawamichiyamisoka'an : Founded around 1716-36, this is an *udon/soba* noodle and Japanese cuisine restaurant in Fuyamachi. The quiet and reserved white linen *noren* has great character. (Kyoto)

76. Gonbei : Gonbei is an *udon* noodle shop in Gion-machi that is specially noted for its *kama'age* noodles. The large lantern, black lattice and black *noren* make an intriguing combination. (Kyoto)

77. Owariya : Founded in 1629, this shop is noted for its *horai soba* and *soba mochi*. Its peaceful exterior and the character "宝" on the front *noren* sets a tranquil scene. (Kyoto)

78. Chagetsu : This *noren* hangs at the front entrance of the combination Japanese restaurant-inn, Chagetsu, near Awataguchi. The plum blossom on the *noren* is exquisite. (Kyoto)

79. Kitaro : This is a *yudofu* restaurant in Gion Shinchi. The simple *noren* blends in beautifully with the rustic exterior. (Kyoto)

80. Ippei Teahouse : The teahouse seems like a setting out of a play. The teahouse serves Kyoto cuisine in a calm and quiet atmosphere. (Kyoto)

81. Okutan : Okutan is near the gate of Nanzenji. This *yudofu* restaurant was founded in early Edo and has prospered for twelve generations. The plain *noren* hangs nobly in front of the simple country-style house. (Kyoto)

82. Junsei : Located near the outermost gate of Nanzenji, Junsei is blessed with a large garden. This is the site where the Junseishoin School was established by a scholar of Western science. It is a *yudofu* restaurant today. (Kyoto)

79 Kitaro

80 Ippei Teahouse

81 Okutan

82 Junsei

83 Matsumaeya

84 Matsumaeya

85 Yaosan

83. Matsumaeya : Established in 1392, this store has a 600-year history in *konbu*, kelp, through thirty-one generations. It takes pride in the "Kinri Goyodokoro" symbol on the white, linen *noren* bestowed by the Imperial House. (Kyoto)

84. Matsumaeya : The store's furnishings and its full-length *noren* create an air of elegance.

85. Yaosan : Established in 1708, Yaosan has been making *yuzu miso* for 270 years. The house was restored to its original state in 1864. It is a typical Kyoto tradesman's house built in the *mushiko* style with projecting lattice. The crest is simple and beautiful. (Kyoto)

86. Honda Miso : This store was founded around 1830-40 and specializes in the white Kyoto-style *miso*. The character "丹" on the front *noren* was the first character of the founder's name. The *noren* goes superbly with the tranquil composure of the old tradesman's house. (Kyoto)

87. Fuka : Founded in the 19th century, this store makes *fu* which is wheat-gluten bread. The building was constructed around 1848-54. The "力" character capped with the mountain crest on the *noren* makes an interesting contrast with the stone bench. (Kyoto)

88. Yubahan : Yubahan has been a maker of Kyoto *yuba* since 1716. The light black ink on the white linen imparts an air of elegance to the *noren* and blends with the old tradesman's house and the bench. (Kyoto)

86 Honda Miso

87 Fuka

88 Yubahan

89 Doi Shibazuke

90 Narita

91 Murakamiju

92 Honode

89. Doi Shibazuke: *Shibazuke* pickles has a history of 1000 years, going back to the Heian Period. But the shop in Ohara was established in 1899. The old storefront and *noren* have a solid sturdiness. (Kyoto)
90. Narita: This store which sells Kyoto-style pickles, *suguki*, is located near Kamikamo Shrine. The simple *noren* goes beautifully with the old-fashioned house. (Kyoto)
91. Murakamiju: Located near Takase River, Murakamiju was established around 1830-44 and makes *senmizuke*. The crest with the character "⊕" was given by the Shimazu family of Satsuma. (Kyoto)
92. Honode: Honode is located on the Kirara slope in Ichijoji Sagarimatsu near Shisendo. It has been making *kirarazuke* since 1689. Long ago it was a teahouse. Today it looks inconspicuous, like a quiet and unobtrusive country house. (Kyoto)
93. Tanakacho: Tanakacho has been making *mirinzuke* for almost two hundred years, dating back to 1789. The 19th century house still retains its old furnishings and appearance. (Kyoto)
94. Yaoi: Yaoi is a *senmaizuke* shop on the corner of Shinbashi in Gion. (Kyoto)
95. Senmaruya: Senmaruya is a Kyoto *yuba* shop in Sakai-cho in Shijo. (Kyoto)
96. Sugukiya Rokurobei: This shop, in front of the *torii* of Kamikamo Shrine, specializes in Kamo-grown *kaburazuke suguki*. (Kyoto)

93 Tanakacho

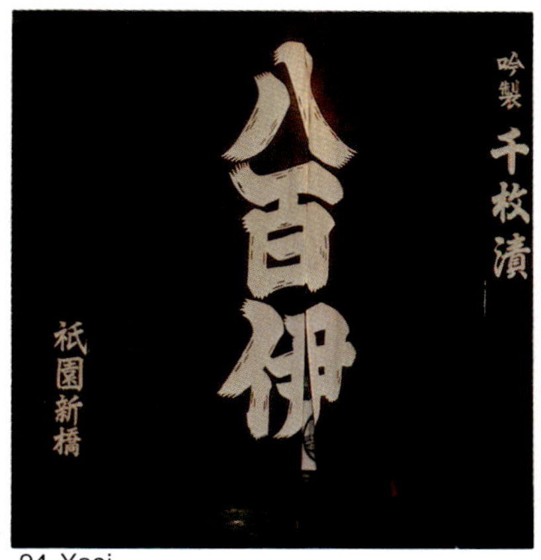

94 Yaoi

95 Senmaruya

96 Sugukiya Rokurobei

97 Shichimiya

98 Ariya

99 Tokubei Masuda

97. Shichimiya: Founded in 1656 and located near the temple Kiyomizudera, this shop has been making *shichimitogarashi* for over three hundred years. (Kyoto)
98. Ariya: In the past Ariya was a Japanese confectionary shop in Kiyamachi. Today it is an *okonomiyaki* shop. The ant motif on the *noren* is very interesting. (Kyoto)
99. Tokubei Masuda: Located near Fushimi, this shop has been brewing *sake* since the 19th century. This is the *noren* of that shop which is known for its cloudy *sake*, *Tsuki-no-katsura*. (Kyoto)
100. Bunnosuke-jaya: The *rakugo* or monologist storyteller Bunnosuke Jr. opened this sweet *sake* teahouse near Kodaiji. (Kyoto)
101. Bunnosuke-jaya: The puffy face of *Otafuku* decorates the *noren* hanging in the teahouse.

100 Bunnosuke-jaya

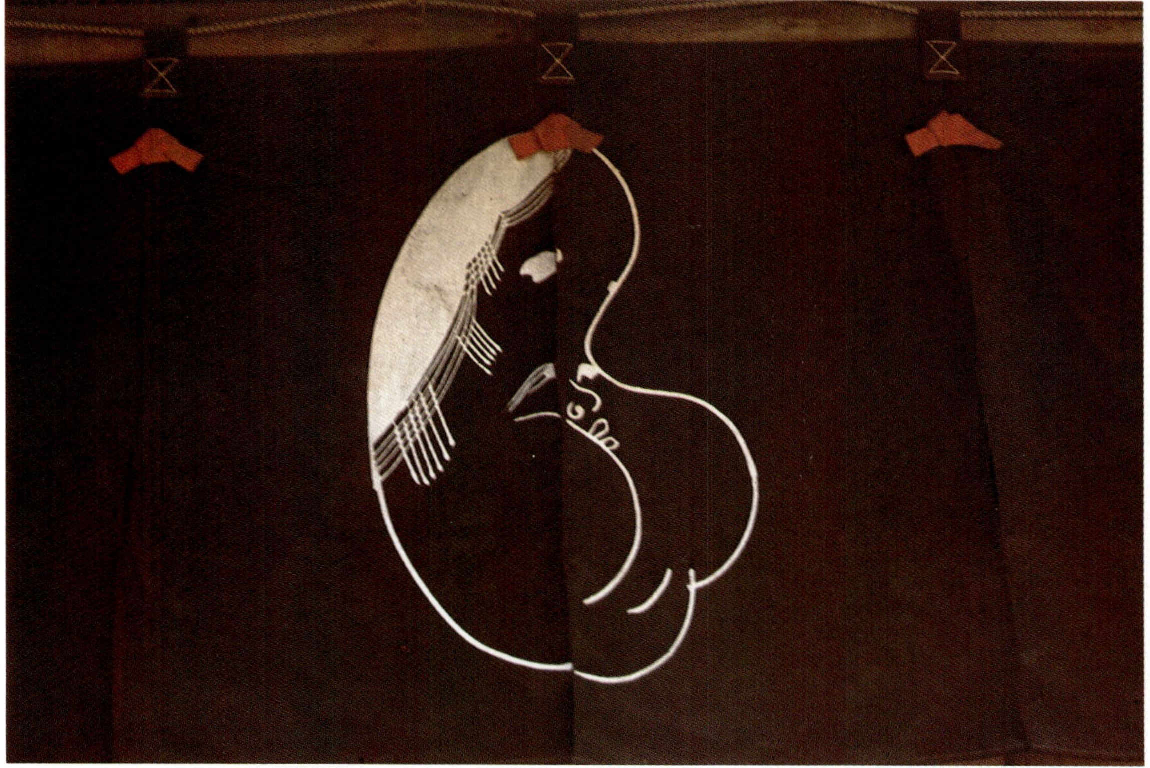

101 Bunnosuke-jaya

102 Kawabata Doki

103 Kawabata Doki

104 Kameya Mutsu

105 Kameya Iori

106 Kameya Kiyonaga

107 Kameya Yoshinaga

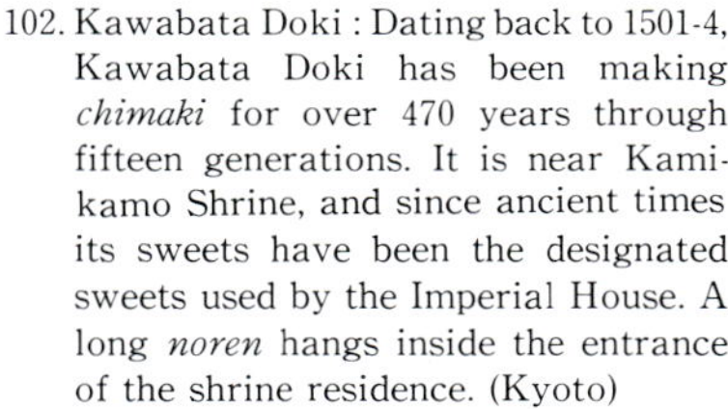

102. Kawabata Doki : Dating back to 1501-4, Kawabata Doki has been making *chimaki* for over 470 years through fifteen generations. It is near Kamikamo Shrine, and since ancient times its sweets have been the designated sweets used by the Imperial House. A long *noren* hangs inside the entrance of the shrine residence. (Kyoto)

103. Kawabata Doki : This full-length *noren* hangs at the doorway to the kitchen.

104. Kameya Mutsu : This Kyoto-style sweets shop founded in 1421 has continued to exist through twenty-one generations with the history of Nishi Honganji. (Kyoto)

105. Kameya Iori : This dried confectionary shop has a 300-year history stretching over seventeen generations to the early 17th century. (Kyoto)

106. Kameya Kiyonaga : Known for its Chinese sweets, *seijo kankidan*, this Kyoto-style sweets shop has been located in Gion Ishidanshita since about the 18th century.(Kyoto)

107. Kameya Yoshinaga : Established in 1832 this Kyoto-style sweet shop is known for *oike senbei* crackers. (Kyoto)

108. Kameya Yoshinaga : A different shop with name pronounced in the same way as No. 107 was established in 1804, this Kyoto-style sweets shop is known for the crackers as well. (Kyoto)

108 Kameya Yoshinaga

109 Kawamichi-ya Sohonke

110 Sasaya Iori

111 Tsuruya Yoshinobu

112 Kamesuehiro

109. Kawamichi-ya Sohonke: This shop has a 320-year history beginning in the 17th century. The shop is located on Anekoji Road and known for *sobaboro* cookies. (Kawamichi)

110. Sasaya Iori: Established in 1716, this is a nine-generation-old Kyoto-style sweets shop in Shichijo Ohmiya. It is noted for the *dorayaki* cakes that are offered on the temple festival day of Kobo Daishi at Tōji. (Kyoto)

111. Tsuruya Yoshinobu: Established in 1718, it is famous for the Japanese sweets called *kyokanze* that have the *kanze* water ring pattern and *yuzu-mochi*. (Kyoto)

112. Kamesuehiro: This dried confectionary shop, founded in 1804, is renowned for *kyo-no-yosuga* and *kamesue dainagon* sweets. The two *noren* coordinate superbly with the imposing structure of the Kyoto-style tradesman's house. (Kyoto)

113 Tobei Matsuya

114 Tawaraya Yoshitomi

115 Tawaraya Yoshitomi

116 Tawaraya Yoshitomi

113. Tobei Matsuya: This Kyoto-style sweets shop founded during the 18th century is located near Daitokuji and known for *Murasaki no matsukaze* sweets. (Kyoto)

114. Tawaraya Yoshitomi: This Kyoto-style sweets shop founded in 1755 is known for *unryu* sweets, a specialty of Kyoto. The straw rice bag is splendidly used as a motif in the *noren*. (Kyoto)

115. 116. Tawaraya Yoshitomi: This is the *noren* at the front entrance and the kitchen.

117. Mamemasa: This store is a retailer of the Kyoto sweets, *goshiki* beans, which are used on auspicious occasions. The design of the birds and beans on the white *noren* hanging in the entrance is charming. (Kyoto)

118. Mamemasa: This is the *noren* at the front entrance.

119. Jurokugo: This is a *goshiki* bean shop across from the Minamiza theater.

120. Surugaya Shimozato: Established in 1818, this shop is noted for *mameheito*. The *noren* hanging over the Gion tradesman's house is modest, however the fringe and design radiate warmth. (Kyoto)

117 Mamemasa

118 Mamemasa

119 Jurokugo

120 Surugaya Shimozato

121 Kagizen Yoshifusa

122 Kagizen Yoshifusa

123 Yatsuhashi Nishio

124 Heianden

125 Shioyoshiken

121. 122. Kagizen Yoshifusa: Kagizen Yoshifusa, a Kyoto-style sweets shop founded during the 19th century, is known for *kuzukiri*. It is located in front of Ichiriki-jaya in Gion. The key design in the *noren* is quite fascinating. (Kyoto)

123. Yatsuhashi Nishio: This shop is near Kumano Shrine and famous for the Kyoto sweets called *yatsuhashi*. (Kyoto)

124. Heianden: This shop is near Heian Shrine and famous for the Kyoto-style sweets called *heianden*. The tile used at the imperial residence at the Heian Palace is employed as a motif here. (Kyoto)

125. Shioyoshiken: This Kyoto-style sweet shop is noted for *juraku manju*. The large *noren* with the products' names dyed in white hanging at the entrance coordinates splendidly with the old-fashioned tradesman's house. (Kyoto)

126. Torayakurokawa: Dating back to the 8th century, this store is very distinguished for Toraya *manju* and is located west of the Kyoto Imperial Palace. The *noren* with the white background hangs proudly over the entrance. (Kyoto)

126 Torayakurokawa

127 Jinbado

128 Aoiya Sohonpo

129 Kogestu

127. Jinbado : Established in 1872, this 100-year old teahouse stands in front of the Kamikamo Shrine. It is famous for *yakimochi*, a Kamo specialty. (Kyoto)
128. Aoiya Sohonpo : This shop, built in the style of a shrine, is known for *yakimochi*. (Kyoto)
129. Kogetsu : This Kyoto-style sweets shop opened a new shop in Arashiyama. The hand-drum on the front *noren* makes an interesting motif. (Kyoto)
130. Sakuraiya : In olden times Sakuraiya was a teahouse near Kitano Shrine well known for its *tsunagi-dango* dumplings. In modern times it has become a rented hall and garage. This photograph was taken ten years ago. (Kyoto)
131. Kazariya : This old teahouse stands at the entrance of Imamiya Shrine and is known for *aburi-mochi*. (Kyoto)
132. 133. Ichimonji-ya (Ichiwa) : It is said to be close to one thousand years old and it is renowned for *aburi-mochi*. Its architecture is that of a typical teahouse. (Kyoto)

130 Sakuraiya

131 Kazariya

132 Ichimonji-ya (Ichiwa)

133 Ichimonji-ya (Ichiwa)

134 Yamabana Sokyudo

135 Honke Sakura-Mochi

136 Kawakami

137 Kinko'an

134. Yamabana Sokyudo : This shop has been popular since olden times for *hato-mochi* and *detchi-yokan* jelly. On its *noren*, it uses the charming motif of a pigeon. (Kyoto)
135. Honke Sakura-Mochi : This shop is located at the corner of Togetsu Bridge in Arashiyama. The *noren* hangs in the annex which is noted for *sakura-mochi*. (Kyoto)
136. Kawakami : This Japanese sweets tea shop is near Kamikamo Shrine. (Kyoto)
137. Kinko'an : This *ohagi* rice dumpling shop is near Nanzenji. (Kyoto)
138. Hararyokaku : Located in Gion, this is the only shop in Japan that sells Gion *kousen* in a bamboo container. Long ago *Kousen* was a drink similar to herb tea. A macramé *noren* hangs inside the old entrance. (Kyoto)
139. Kichikudo : This shop has been said to specialize in bamboo ware since the end of the 19th century. The contrast of the imitation bamboo front exterior and the *noren* is effective. (Kyoto)
140. Kawasaki : During the Edo Period it was a money changers' shop called Zeniya Shinbei. Later it handled Japanese-type paper. It is now in its eighth generation. The *noren* used during the time it was a money changers is still hanging inside the entrance. (Kyoto)

138 Hararyokaku

139 Kichikudo

140 Kawasaki

141 Kyo Horiya

142 Tomatsuya

143 Nakayama Doll Shop

141. Kyo Horiya : The modest *noren* and the old lantern combine well with the Kyoto townhouse which is a wooden doll shop. (Kyoto)

142. Tomatsuya : This shop has been making Noh fans since about the 19th century. Today, it still makes fans for various schools of Noh. A large motif of a fan fills the *noren*. (Kyoto)

143. Nakayama Doll Shop : Established in 1657, it uses the "Ashidaya" as the store's trademark. It makes Kyoto dolls for the Boy's and Girl's Festivals in Kyoto. The shop is proud of its 300-year history. (Kyoto)

144. Jusan-ya : The numbers 9 and 4 for combs are added to total 13, giving the store its name Jusan-ya. This is a *suge* comb store. A comb and hair ornament are beautifully used as a motif on the small *noren*. (Kyoto)

145. Kinchikudo : This store in Gion sells eyebrow pencils, brushes, lip rouge and other traditional cosmetics used since ancient times. (Kyoto)

146. Fundo-ya : This *tabi* footwear shop was established around 1854-60. The craftmanship of handmade *tabi* has been passed down from generation to generation for over one hundred years. (Kyoto)

147. Choboya : Choboya is a long established footwear store in Gion which makes high wooden clogs for the *Maiko* dancers. The *chobo* dot makes an interesting motif on the *noren*. (Kyoto)

144 Jusan-ya

145 Kinchikudo

146 Fundo-ya

147 Choboya

148 Konjaku

149 Okakimi

150 Hatsusegawa

151 Tachikichi

152 Tanbaya

148. Konjaku: This shop is known for its indigo dyeing of traditonal old fabrics and bags. The characters on the *noren* are fascinating. (Kyoto)

149. Okakimi: This dainty, picturesque shop is near Gion Jūnidanya teahouse. The brownish, orange-dyed *noren* is exquisite. (Kyoto)

150. Hatsusegawa: This is a lacquerware store in Takatsuji Yanagi-baba. The distinctive motif of the spool has a crisp, fresh look. (Kyoto)

151. Tachikichi: This fifteen-generation-old pottery shop in Tomikoji in Shinjuku was founded in 1752. Its former name was Tachibanaya Kichibei. The white mandarin blossom on the *noren*, chosen from the name Tachibana meaning mandarin blossom, is bold and feminine. (Kyoto)

152. 155. Tanbaya: This antique store near Kumano Shrine is known for its collection of utensils for *soba* liquid including bowls, pots, and jars. (Kyoto)

153. Yasushige: This is a cutlery shop on Horikawa Avenue in Sanjo. (Kyoto)

154. Marusan-honpo: This is a unique Kyoto "Shikkaiya" known for *kongo kurozome* black dye. The store name, Marusan, designating three bars in a circle is simple and beautiful. (Kyoto)

153 Yasushige

154 Marusan-honpo

155 Tanbaya

156 Sanshibo

157 Tenpyodo

156. Sanshibo: This is a pottery shop in Kawaramachi in Sanjo. The simple *noren* looks striking against the row of pottery lined up against the house. (Kyoto)

157. Tenpyodo: This antique shop is on Shin-Monzen Street. (Kyoto)

158. Inoue Drugs: The striking *noren* with the parallel crosses hangs in the inner garden. Established in 1705, the store deals in eyewashes and eye lotions. (Kyoto)

159. Amamori: Founded in 1648, it is the fourteenth generation of Amamori which specializes in salves and ointments. (Kyoto)

160. Hata Drugs: This twelfth-generation herb medicine store is known for *kiogan*. (Kyoto)

158 Inoue Drugs

159 Amamori

160 Hata Drugs

161 Arakawa-Family

162 Ubagamochi Yorotei

163 Kobaien

161. Arakawa-Family: This townhouse built like an old farmhouse is near Daitokuji. The plain bamboo *noren* is exquisite. (Kyoto)

162. Ubagamochi Yorotei: This is located at Kusatsu which was depicted as one of the 53 Tokaido stations. Shown here is the *noren* hanging from the eaves of a teahouse known for *ubagamochi*. (Kusatsu)

163. Kobaien: This ink shop in Nara is over four hundred years old and goes back fourteen generations to around 1573. It is said that since the time of founder, Matsui Dochin, the old procedure of preparing *sumi* ink is still being observed. The *noren* hangs with distinction in the recesses of the townhouse. (Nara)

164. Kobaien: This is the *noren* seen from the inner garden.

164 Kobaien

165 Genrin-do

165. Genrin-do : Founded in 1717, this is a *Narazumi* ink shop. The small *noren* hanging in the recesses of the old tradesman's house is simple and beautiful. (Nara)

166 Yanagi- chaya

167 Yanagi-chaya

168 Tono-chaya

166. Yanagi-chaya : This restaurant is known for *kaiseki* cuisine and Nara *chameshi* rice. Shown here is the linen *noren* of the restaurant beside Sarusawa Pond. (Nara)

167. Yanagi-chaya : This is the macramé *noren* of the restaurant near Tono-chaya.

168. Tono-chaya : This tea shop is located at the foot of the five-storied pagoda at Kofukuji. The simple, white *noren* suits the shop beautifully. It is built like a tea cermony room. (Nara)

169. 170. Hiraso : It is said that *Kaki-no-hazushi* was presented to the royal family in the 14th century by the villagers of Kawakami village in Okuyoshino. The front and inside entrance *noren* of Hiraso are pictured here. Hiraso was transferred from Yoshino to Nara. (Nara)

171. Imanishi Narazuke : The history of *Narazuke* pickles is said to go back to the Nara Period. Established in the late 19th century on Sanjo Avenue, Imanishi Narazuke is over one hundred years old. (Nara)

172. 173. Mori-Narazuke Shop : These are front and inside entrance *noren* of the Mori-Narazuke shop. Located in front of Todaiji in Nara, this shop is over one hundred years old. (Nara)

169 Hiraso

170 Hiraso

171 Imanishi Narazuke

172 Mori-Narazuke Shop

173 Mori-Narazuke Shop

174.175. Zeitakumame-honpo : This bean confectionary store is located on Sanjo Avenue. The white awning *noren* is refreshing against the old tradesman's house. (Nara)

176. Manmando : Established in 1868, this shop sells Chinese *manju* which is one of the sweets received from China by the Kasuga Shrine in about the 10th century. (Nara)

177. Kogetsu : This shop has made and sold only *mikasa-yaki* for the last seventy years. (Nara)

178. Yumeido : This is a typical Nara resting spot for drinking powdered green tea, *matcha*. The white walls and the colored *noren* make a beautiful contrast. (Nara)

179. Chiyonoya Takemura : Founded around 1688-1704 and located on East Mukai Street, this shop has close to a 300-year-old history. It is known for *aoniyoshi*. (Nara)

180. 181. Chiyonoya Takemura : On the left the image of bamboo is used as a character. A sparrow design is used on the right. Both designs are stylish and uncomplicated. (Nara)

174 Zeitakumame-honpo

175 Zeitakumame-honpo

176 Manmando

177 Kogetsu

178 Yumeido

179 Chiyonoya Takemura

180 Chiyonoya Takemura

181 Chiyonoya Takemura

182 Kikuya

183 Kyotomi

184 Kitcho

185 Kitcho

182. Kikuya: Built over four hundred years ago, this shop is famous for *Oshiro-no-kuchimochi*, a specialty of Yamato Koriyama. The white *noren* at the back of the house harmonizes beautifully with the old tradesman's house. (Yamato Koriyama)
183. Kyotomi: This is the front *noren* of a Japanese restaurant-inn in a former pleasure area. The white paulownia on a light yellow background is refreshing. (Yamato Koriyama)
184. Kitcho: Osaka's leading Japanese restaurant; the *noren* made of gourds displays a unique beauty. (Osaka)
185. Kitcho: This gourd *noren* leads to the doorway of the kitchen. (Osaka)

186 Yamato-ya

187 Kitamura

188 Hisanoya

189 Sushi-man

186. Yamato-ya : An elegantly colored *noren* hangs at the front entrance of Yamato-ya, a leading restaurant in south Osaka. (Osaka)

187. Kitamura : Founded in 1881, this four-generation-old restaurant is the originator of Osaka *sukiyaki*. The writing on the right of the *noren* is quite unusual. (Osaka)

188. Hisanoya : This is the front *noren* of Hisanoya in south Osaka which is known for *shabu-shabu*. The gourds make a charming design on the *noren*. (Osaka)

189. Sushi-man : Established in 1653, this fourteen-generation-old restaurant was designated a *sushi* shop for the Imperial House. It has been known since early times for *kodai-suzumezushi*. Escaping fires and wars, the old townhouse goes wonderfully well with the brownish-orange *noren* at its front entrance. (Osaka)

190. Hishitomi : This *noren* leads to the kitchen doorway of Hishitomi, an eel restaurant in Soemon-cho. Prior to the War, Hisanoya was the originator of Edo-style *kabayaki* in Osaka. (Osaka)

190 Hishitomi

191 Kobian

192 Mimiu

193 Imai

194 Shobentangotei

191. Kobian : Kobian specializes in mud-turtle dishes. The bamboo trees growing along the front exterior and the plain *noren* create a subtle and unobtrusive effect. (Osaka)
192. Mimiu : This Japanese restaurant has a 200-year-old history in Sakai. In 1924 it changed its name to the present one. It is known for meals accompanied with *udon* noodles. (Osaka)
193. Imai : In the past, this shop was the Imai Musical Instruments Store. However, it long since became popular as an *udon* and *soba* noodle shop. (Osaka)
194. Shobentangotei : From early times Shobentangotei has been a well-known eating house on Hozenji Yokocho Street. The contrast between *noren* and stone in front of the restaurant, on which the novelist Sakunosuke Oda wrote, is quite appealing. (Osaka)
195. Takoume : This is the front *noren* of Takoume founded in 1844. Its savory dishes of *oden*, Akashi octopus, and whale tongue are widely known. (Osaka)
196. Eho : This is a local Dotonbori cuisine restaurant where many folkcraft goods from Okinawa are gathered for display. The *noren* used in the restaurant is a magnificent "Bingata" *noren* with the symbol of a phoenix. (Osaka)

195 Takoume

196 Eho

197 Matsumoto

198 Daikoku

200 Oguraya-Yamamoto

199 Otora

197. Matsumoto : This is the front *noren* of a small Japanese restaurant in Sonezaki Shinchi. The drawing of a pine is very tasteful. (Osaka)

198. Daikoku : This restaurant has existed for seventy years. Its *kayaku-meshi* rice is very popular. This is the front *noren* of the restaurant. (Osaka)

199. Otora : This is a *kamaboko*, fishcake, shop in Nanba Shinchi. (Osaka)

200. Oguraya-Yamamoto : Founded in 1848, Oguraya-Yamamoto has dealt only in *konbu*, kelp, for 150 years through three generations. It is known as the setting for Toyoko Yamazaki's novel, "*Noren*". (Osaka)

201. 202. Oguraya-Yamamoto : These are the *noren* in the kitchen (left) and inside the entrance (right) .

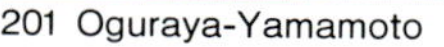
201 Oguraya-Yamamoto

202 Oguraya-Yamamoto

203 Terashima Sohonten

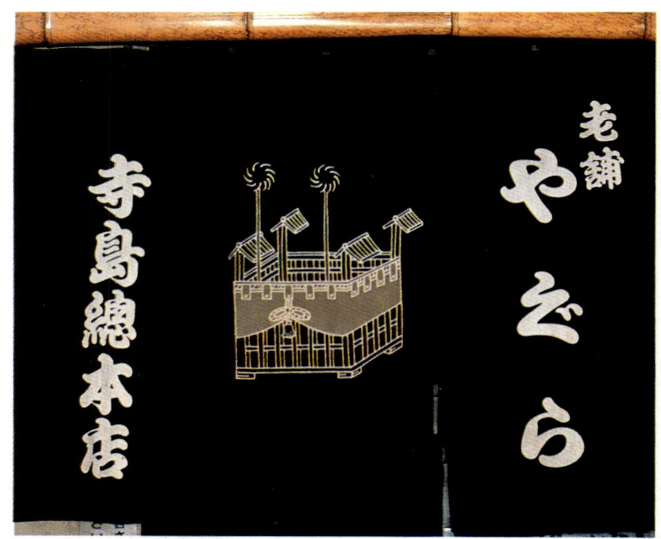

204 Terashima Sohonten

205 Tsuruya Hachiman

206 Tachibanaya Juei

207 Tsunosei

208 Tsunosei

203. Terashima Sohonten: This is one of the top three *kuriokoshi* makers. This is the front *noren* of Terashima Sohonten in Dotonbori, known long for *yaguraokoshi*. (Osaka)

204. Terashima Sohoten: The drawing of a decorative scaffold on the *noren* inside the entrance is very unusual. (Osaka)

205. Tsuruya Hachiman: This *noren* hangs inside the entrance of Tsuruya Hachiman. Established in 1869, it has been noted for its steamed confections since early times. The crane motif is very lovely. (Osaka)

206. Tachibanaya Juei: Founded in 1716, this *okoshi* shop is 260 years old, spanning nine generations. The *noren* over the kitchen doorway is splendid with the outline of a fan and the character "橘" adorning it. (Osaka)

207. 208. Tsunosei: This shop was founded in 1752. Hearing the words, Futatsu Ido, we think of *iwaokoshi*. This *noren* hangs inside Tsunosei which has the longest history for *kuriokoshi*. (Osaka)

209. Tsunosei: This is the front exterior of Tsunosei which has two wells. Therefore, the best water in Osaka must be from these two wells.

209 Tsunosei

210 Shirusei

211 Naniwa Zenzai

212 Amanoya

213 Meotozenzai

210. Shirusei: This shop serves *kayaku-meshi* rice and soups. Like a stage setting, it has a playfulness to it. (Osaka)

211. Naniwa Zenzai: Although it is a new Japanese sweets tea shop in Midosuji, the emblem on the *noren* is very attractive. (Osaka)

212. Amanoya: Amanoya is a new Japanese sweets tea shop opened about sixty years ago. The design of the *noren* leading to the kitchen is neat and simple. (Osaka)

213. Meotozenzai: The Meotozenzai tea-house next to the Mizukake Fudo Temple in Hozenji is said to be 115 years old. One *zenzai* is served in two bowls to couples. Though a small shop, it became famous in the work of the novelist, Sakunosuke Oda. (Osaka)

中国

Chugoku District

1 Koeido Takeda

2 Izutsuya

3 Mori Liquor Store

4 Kikkodo

1. Koeido Takeda: Founded in 1856, this store makes *kibidango* dumplings, an Okayama specialty. Permission was given by the former liege lord to use the Bizenkoku seal of Kuginuki. (Okayama)
2. Izutsuya: This is the front *noren* of a quick-lunch restaurant built in the ancient traditional style of old Japan. (Okayama)
3. Mori Liquor Store: This old liquor store faces the Kurashiki River. The sun-shielding bamboo blind and the left and right front *noren* harmonize beautifully. (Kurashiki)
4. Kikkodo: This is the front exterior of the over 100-year-old Kikkodo. Dating back to 1868, it is famous for the confection, *murasuzume*. (Kurashiki)
5. Kikkodo: In old Japan before the Nara Period, fruit, primarily the mandarin orange, was considered a sweet. As a result, the mandarin blossom derived from the store name became the trademark of this *noren*.
6. Shinkawa: This is the front *noren* of Shinkawa, a restaurant facing the Kurashiki River that is noted for *tenryo udon*. (Kurashiki)
7. Azumi: This is the kitchen *noren* of Azumi, a shop facing the Kurashiki River that is known for the Shinshu Naito style of hand-kneaded *soba* noodles. (Kurashiki)

5 Kikkodo

6 Shinkawa

7 Azumi

8 Hashimaya

9 Shuto'en

8. Hashimaya: This 110-year-old kimono shop spans over five generations going back to 1869. The front *noren* uses the first character of the founder's name, Tokuyoshi, as a motif for the *noren*. (Kurashiki)

9. Shuto'en: This folkcraft kiln facing the Kurashiki River specializes in pottery called Bizenyaki. The wooden lattice and the *noren* hanging down from the eaves make an attractive combination. (Kurashiki)

10 Yano Dried Food Store

11 Takahashi Tea Shop

12 Takahashi Tea Shop

10. Yano Dried Food Store: Established in early Edo, this old house has contiuned to stand for three hundred years in Yonago City. The *noren* is simple and beautiful, using the character "の" plus arrow feathers. (Yonago)

11. 12. Takahashi Tea Shop: This tea shop dates back to the 17th century. The tea kettle and other tea utensils are used in the *noren*. (Yonago)

13. 14. Kawabata Seihachi: This is the *noren* in the restaurant of Kawabata Seihachi that is famous for Matsuba crab, a Japan sea specialty. (Yonago)

15. Sato Paper Store: This fifteen generation- old shop was established during the 18th century and is over two hundred years old. Japanese ginger is used as the motif in the shop's *noren*. (Onomichi)

13 Kawabata Seihachi

15 Sato Paper Store

14 Kawabata Seihachi

16 Kososhi

17 Kososhi

18 Kigaru

19 Yagumo Honjin

16. 17. Kososhi : This is a new shop of Izumo *soba* noodles that is housed in a modest townhouse. The top *noren* is an Izumo indigo-dyed *furoshiki* cloth. The front *noren* that is made from a *hanten* jacket is interesting. (Matsue)

18. Kigaru : The store name is taken from the expression "kigaru" in which the *daruma* will not fall down left or right. This is the front *noren* of Kigaru which is known for *wariko soba*. (Matsue)

19. Yagumo Honjin : The building was constructed in 1733 on the old road in Izumo and was designated the official *daimyo* inn. Succeeding for fourteen generations, this is the oldest house in the district. This large Izumo indigo-dyed *noren* that was used as a divider separating the entrance from the interior is beautifully decorated with linking rings. (Shinji)

20 Izutsuya

21 Osada Dye Shop

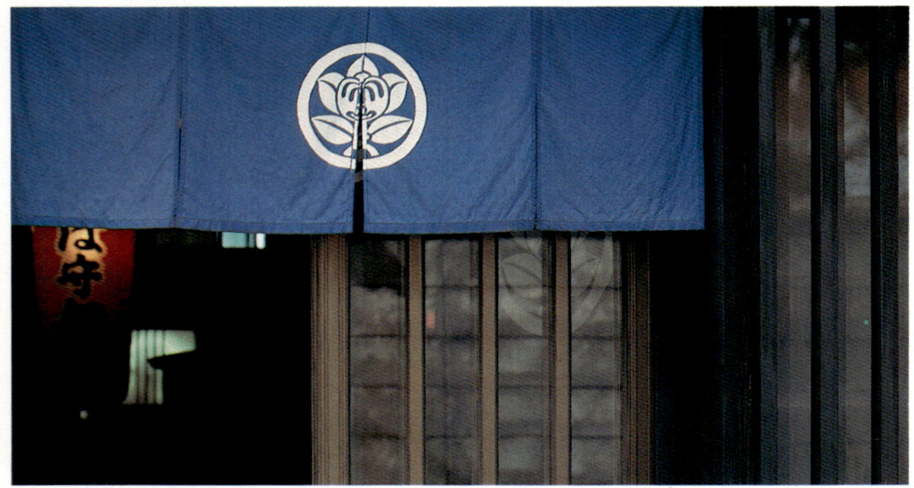

22 Kagi

20. Izutsuya: This has been an Izumo indigo-dye shop since the 19th century. (Izumo)

21. Osada Dye Shop: This Izumo indigo shop is located at the foot of Kaminari Bridge over the Takase River in Izumo. It is a custom throughout Izumo that the bridal *furoshiki* is indigo-dyed. (Izumo)

22. Kagi: Although this is a relatively new store noted for Izumo and *wariko soba*, the indigo-dyed *noren* is gorgeous. (Izumo)

四国
Shikoku Distric

1 Sanuki Mingeikan

2 Komatsutei

5 Waraya

3 Kutsuwado Soke

4 Kanaizumi

1. Sanuki Mingeikan: This is the *noren* in the Prefectural Folkcraft Museum that opened in 1965 in Ritsurin Park. The motif of an ancient Japanese coin is magnificent. (Takamatsu)
2. Komatsutei: This linen *noren* was found at a rest station tea shop in Ritsurin Park. The shape of the gourd is very charming. (Takamatsu)
3. Kutsuwado Soke: This is the *noren* in Kutsuwado Soke founded in 1868. It is known for *kawara senbei* rice crackers that use locally grown sugar beet. The horse bit makes an interesting motif. (Takamatsu)
4. Kanaizumi: This is the front *noren* of Kanaizumi which is noted for *Sanuki-udon* noodle, a local specialty. The contrast of Sakabayashi made from cedar leaves that can be seen on the eaves is interesting. (Takamatsu)
5. Waraya: This is at the entrance of Shikoku Village, constructed a few years ago at southern foot of Mt. Yashima. This Zaigo *udon* noodle house was moved here from Tokushima East Soya Village, and its rustic beauty was preserved. (Yashima)

6. Sanuki-udon: This is the front *noren* of a shop near Takamatsu station that serves *Sanuki-udon*, the local specialty. (Takamatsu)

7. Kume Family: The former residence of Tsuken Kume, the most prominent scientist in the 19th century, was moved from Umajuku, Hikita-cho, Kagawa Prefecture to Shikoku Village. The Shikoku kite and the *noren* make an attractive combination. (Yashima)

6 Sanuki-udon

7 Kume Family

8 Toraya

9 Ishidanya

8. Toraya: Established in 1690, it has been about three hundred years since the old house became an official *daimyo* inn. In the beginning it brewed *sake* for the Konpira Shrine's use. Later it became an inn. You can feel the history behind this building even in the kitchen *noren*. (Kotohira)
9. Ishidanya: During the 19th century it was an inn called Asadaya Kyuhachi. It was also a place for moxibustion. Now in its sixth generation, the house is known as Kyuman. The harmony between the simple *noren* and the antique store sign is marvelous. (Kotohira)
10. Hogetsudo: This is the awning of a shop known for *rokumangoku* and *kyogoku*, local sweets of Marugame City. (Marugame)
11. Fumio: This new *noren* was in the kitchen of a folk sweets shop. You can sense the local design patterns in this Awa dance. (Marugame)

12. 13. Hinodero: This *noren* is in the shop of Hinodero which was founded in 1852 and is famous for *wafu-yokan* jelly. The seaweed motif makes a striking *noren*. (Tokushima)

10 Hogetsudo

11 Fumio

12 Hinodero

13 Hinodero

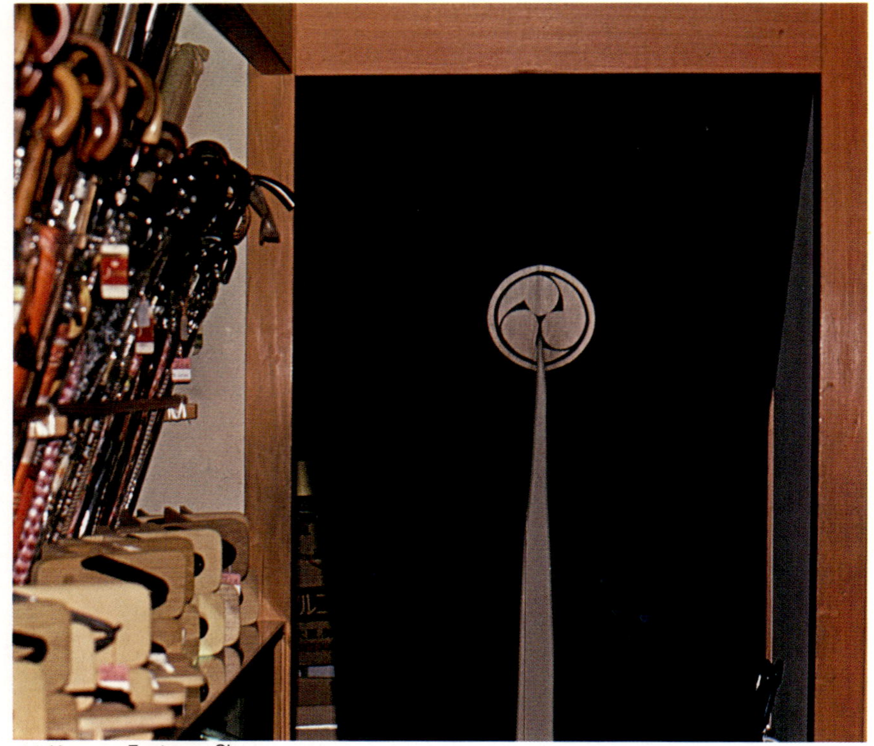

14 Hazama Footwear Shop

15 Hisaroku

16 Tosahan

17 Ikezawa

14. Hazama Footwear Shop: This is the *noren* inside Hazama that began in the late 19th century with the *samurai* of the Tosa clan. (Kochi)
15. Hisaroku: This is the *noren* inside Hisaroku that is known for kites and Shikoku folkcrafts. (Takamatsu)
16. Tosahan: Although it is a new store, it is famous for Tosa cuisine. The single character for fish "魚" used as a motif is striking. (Kochi)
17. Ikezawa: This is the *noren* inside Ikezawa which is known for eel, live fish dishes, and catering. (Kochi)

九州
Kyushu District

1 Nakanishi Hakata-Ori

2 Nakanishi Hakata-Ori

3 Matsuya

1. 2. Nakanishi Hakata-Ori: In 1600 when Nagamasa Kuroda became feudal lord, he declared that Hakata-Ori fabric should be presented to the shogunate. From then on the name Kenjo Hakata-Ori has existed. However, as one of the twelve appointed weavers of the feudal clan, Nakanishi Hakata-Ori has been a weaver for the last century. The top and bottom are *noren* inside the store. (Fukuoka)

3. Matsuya: Established around 1670-81, Matsuya was appointed the confectioner by the former Kuroda clan. The swirl of the Japanese wisteria against a white background was the Kuroda family crest and permission to use it was received from the third generation, Lord Mitsuyuki. This is the awning of Matsuya known for its egg-*somen* sweets. (Fukuoka)

4. 5. Shin-Miura: Established in 1910, Shin-Miura is noted for *mizutaki*, a Hakata specialty. When I was in the navy, the send-off party of the naval school was held there. The faded *noren* was the same as I had fondly remembered from those days. (Fukuoka)

4 Shin-Miura

6. Fujiyoshi: These are the inside and front *noren* of a *yaki-tori* restaurant set in quiet, traditional surroundings. (Fukuoka)

7. Kawasho: This is a *sushi* shop in Nishi-Nakasu famous for the wonderful taste of mackerel *sushi*. The store name taken from a Kabuki play is dyed in large characters on the *noren*. (Fukuoka)

5 Shin-Miura

6 Fujiyoshi

7 Kawasho

8 Shirayukido Etsuzan

9 Konomien

8. Shirayukido Etsuzan: This is the *noren* in Shirayukido Etsuzan, founded in 1855, which makes Etsuzan-mochi, a Yanagawa specialty. (Yanagawa)

9. Konomien: This is a simple front *noren* of Konomien which is known for *yame* tea, an Okihata specialty. (Yanagawa)

10. Shogetsu: Shogetsu is a Japanese restaurant and inn located in Yanagawa. As written in Hakushu Kitahara's poem, Kaigetsuro, was in the pleasure area in the 19th century. From early times Shogetsu and Wakamatsuya have been known for their *unagi-meshi* rice and are very popular among writers. The characters written on the kitchen *noren* are beautiful. (Yanagawa)

11. Otsu Kamaboko-main store: This is the kitchen *noren* of Otsu Kamaboko which is a famous for *daimyo kamaboko*, fish cake, a Yanagawa specialty.

12. Akune: By renovating an old local house, Akune became a Japanese restaurant and inn. As the *noren* casts a mood of serenity, its quiet and unassuming appearance reminds one of a teahouse at the old relay station. (Yanagawa)

13. Tsuruya: Founded in 1639, it is a more than 330-year-old Japanese sweet shop in Saga. The stylish motif of a crane against a white background graces the *noren* in the shop. (Saga)

14. Matsukawaya: Matsukawaya has existed from about the 17th century in the prosperous town of Shin-Baba which was the shrine town of Matsubara Shrine that worshipped the ancestors of the Nabeshima clan. It is a Japanese restaurant and inn long known for Ariake cuisine such as *mutsugoro*. The pine motif in the *noren* is very intriguing. (Saga)

10 Shogetsu

11 Otsu Kamaboko-main store

12 Akune

13 Tsuruya

14 Matsukawaya

15. 17. Oharashinise: Founded in 1850, this shop is noted for *shoro manju*, a Karatsu specialty. On the left and right are shown *noren* from inside the store. The simple pine design is refined, projecting a solid appearance. (Karatsu)

16. Fujio Brewery: This is the front *noren* of Fujio Brewery known for *Sakai Masamune*, a local Karatsu brand. (Karatsu)

18. Yoyokaku: This is a Japanese restaurant and inn established in 1861. It was originally a brothel, and there are many colorful vestiges of that time remaining today. The lattice of the front exterior and awning *noren* radiate a bright freshness. (East Karatsu)

15 Oharashinise

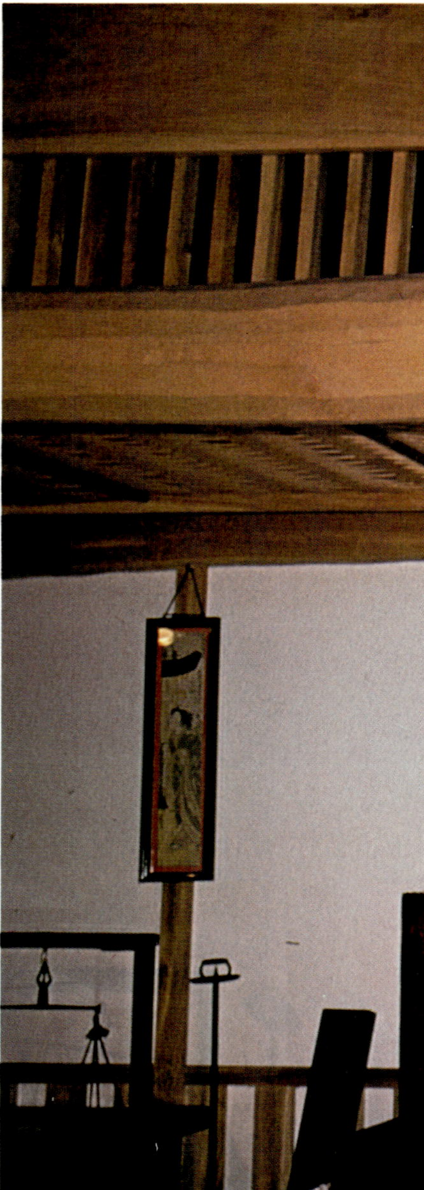
17 Oharashinise

16 Fujio Brewery

18 Yoyokaku

19 Iwanaga Baijuken

20 Yosso

21 Yosso

22 Fukusaya

23 Fukusaya

19. Iwanaga Baijuken : This is an awning *noren* of Iwanaga Baijuken that was founded in 1830 and is famous for *kangiku*, a Nagasaki speciality. (Nagasaki)

20. 21. Yosso : Yosso dates back to 1866 and is known for *chawanmushi*, steamed custard. The top photo shows the *noren* in the eating house and the bottom one depicts the *noren* hanging over the front entrance. The large red lantern and the white *noren* make an interesting contrast. (Nagasaki)

22. Fukusaya : Founded in 1624, this is the front *noren* of Fukusaya known for Nagasaki sponge cake which was introduced by the Portuguese. (Nagasaki)

23. Fukusaya : There is an intriguing bat motif on the *noren* in the store. (Nagasaki)

24 Kagestu

25 Kagetsu

26 Fukiro

24. Kagetsu : Established in 1642, it was a brothel in Maruyama called Hikitaya which was in the pleasure quarters of Nagasaki. In 1818, it became Kagetsu and was familiar to the *samurai* and scholars of the later 19th century. It is a high-class historic restaurant where Ryoma Sakamoto left his sword mark or where the song "Harusame" was created. This is the lovely *noren* with the motif of a delicate plum blossom inside the entrance. (Nagasaki)
25. Kagetsu : This is the full-length *noren* in the hall on the second floor. (Nagasaki)
26. Fukiro : With over a 300-year-history from the Edo period this restaurant is known for *shippoku* cuisine. In the past its name was Senshutei and was changed to its present name by Ito Hirobumi in the 1870s. A small *noren* adorned with a white peony blossom against a brownish orange background hangs elegantly over the kitchen doorway. (Nagasaki)

Kana-syllable Index

(A)
Aizu Aoi [sweets shop] Aizu Wakamatsu ·········24
Akafuku Honpo [sweets shop] Ise ············84
Akune [inn, restaurant] Yanagawa ·········171
Amamori [druggist] Kyoto ·····················133
Amanoya [sweets shop] Tokyo ···············45
Amanoya [sweets, teahouse] Osaka ·········152
Ando Brewery [*miso* shop] Kakunodate ······18
Aoiya Sohonpo [rice cake shop] Kyoto ···124
Aoyagi Sohonke [sweets shop] Nagoya······84
Arakawa [old family] Kyoto ················134
Ariya [*okonomiyaki* shop] ························114
Azumi [noodle shop] Kurashiki ···············155
(B)
Baikatei [rice cake shop] Tokyo···············42
Baren [teahouse] Takayama·····················72
Bunnosuke-jaya [*amazake* shop] Kyoto ···115
(C)
Chagetsu [inn, restaurant] Kyoto ············108
Chikiriya [*kimono* shop] Kyoto··················89
Chikusen [*kimono* shop] Tokyo ···············31
Chiso [*kimono* shop] Kyoto ·····················88
Chiyonoya Takemura [sweets shop] Nara ··129
Choboya [footwear shop] Kyoto ············129
Chojiya [restaurant] Shizuoka Maruko ······81
Chomeiji Sakuramochi [rice cake shop] Tokyo ··43
Chotakubo [wood carving shop] Takayama ··77
(D)
Daichi [restaurant] Kyoto ·····················105
Daikoku [restaurant] Osaka·····················148
Daikokuya [restaurant] Tokyo··················37
Daikokuya [folkcraft shop] Magome ·········65
Daimonya [*kimono* shop] Echizen Ono ······62
Daisho [dyeing & weaving shop] Kyoto ···93
Doi Shibazuke [pickle shop] Kytoto ·········112
Domyo [braided cord shop] Tokyo ············31
Doraku [restaurant] Kyoto ·····················100
(E)
Ebiya [restaurant] Aizu Wakamatsu ·········27
Ebiya [*tsukudani* shop] Tokyo ·················34
Edomasa [restaurant] Tokyo ··················41
Eho [restaurant] Osaka···························147
Enomotoen [rice cracker shop] Tokyo ······45
(F)
Fujio Brewery [*sake* brewer] Karatsu ······172
Fujiya [towel shop] Tokyo························33
Fujiyoshi [restaurant] Fukuoka ···············169
Fuka [*fu* shop] Kyoto ····························111
Fukiro [restaurant] Nagasaki ··················176
Fukusaya [sponge cake shop] Nagasaki ···175
Fumio [sweets, teahouse] Mamugame ······165
Fumiyo [restaurant] Kyoto························95
Fumuroya [*fu* shop] Kanazawa··················49
Funabashiya [*kuzu-mochi* shop] ···············43
Funasaka Brewery [*sake* brewer] Takayama ··75
Fundoya [*tabi* shop] Kyoto ····················129
(G)
Genrindo [*sumi* ink shop] Nara ···············136
Goemon [restaurant] Tokyo······················40
Gonbei [noodle shop] Kyoto ·················108
Goriya [restaurant] Kanazawa···················55
Goto [used furniture shop] Yonezawa ······22
Gozaku Morihisa [general shop] Morioka ·········20
(H)
Habutae [dumpling shop] Tokyo ·············42
Hanaya [sweets, teahouse] Tokyo ············45
Haneda Brewery [*sake* brewer] Tsuruoka Oyama ···21
Harada Brewery [*sake* brewer] Takayama·········75
Hararyokaku [*kousen* shop] Kyoto ············127
Hashimaya [*kimono* shop] Kurashiki ······156
Hata [druggist] Kyoto ··························133
Hatsusegawa [lacquerware shop] Kyoto ·········130
Hayashiya [tea shop] Kanazawa ················49
Hazama [footwear shop] Kochi ···············166
Heianden [sweets shop] Kyoto ···············122
Hida Minzoku Kokokan [folk art museum] Takayama ·······································68
Higoya [dyeing and weaving shop] Kyoto ·········90
Hiiragiya [inn] Kyoto ·····························97
Hinodero [sweets shop] Tokushima ·········165
Hiranoya [restaurant] Kyoto ····················99
Hiranoya [restaurant] Kyoto ··················103
Hirasawa [old family] Kanazawa ············59
Hirase Brewery [*sake* brewer] Takayama ·········75
Hiraso [*sushi* shop] Nara ······················139
Hisadaya [inn] Takayama ························69
Hisago [restaurant] Tokyo ···················40
Hisanoya [restaurant] Osaka ················144
Hisaroku [folkcraft shop] Takamatsu ······166
Hishitomi [restaurant] Osaka ·················145
Hogetsudo [sweets shop] Marugame ······165
Honda Miso [*miso* shop] Kyoto ···············111
Honode [pickle shop] Kyoto ··················113
Hyotanya [ivory-work shop] Tokyo ·········33
Hyotei [restaurant] Kyoto ·····················103
(I)
Ibishiya [*kimono* shop] Yonezawa ············22
Ichiriki [restaurant] Kyoto ························95
Ichimonjiya (Ichiwa) [rice cake shop] Kyoto ··125
Iemotoya [teahouse] Tokyo ····················44
Ikedaya [druggist] Toyama ·····················62
Ikezawa [restaurant] Kochi ······················166
Ikkyu [restaurant] Kyoto ·······················102
Imai [noodle shop] Osaka ························146
Imoju [sweet potato shop] Kawagoe ········46
Imanishi Narazuke [pickle shop] Nara ···139
Inoue [druggist] Kyoto ···························133
Ippei-jaya [restaurant] Kyoto ················109

Ippodo [tea shop] Kyoto ……87
Iseki [restaurant] Tokyo ……38
Isetatsu [paper shop] Tokyo ……32
Ishibashiya [sweets shop] Sendai ……23
Ishidanya [sweets shop] Kotohira ……164
Ishigura [footwear shop] Yonezawa ……22
Ishikawa [*kimono* shop] Kyoto ……91
Iwanaga Baijuken [sweets shop] Nagasaki 174
Iwata [*kimono* shop] Kyoto ……91
Izuei [restaurant] Tokyo ……37
Izukura [*kimono* shop] Kyoto ……91
Izutsuya [restaurant] Okayama ……154
Izutsuya [dyeing shop] Izumo ……160
Izuu [sushi shop] Kyoto ……107

(J)

Jinbado [rice cake shop] Kyoto ……124
Jinbei [restaurant] Kanazawa ……55
Junsei [restaurant] Kyoto ……109
Juichiya [restaurant] Kyoto ……105
Junidanya [restaurant] Kyoto ……107
Jurokugo [sweets shop] Kyoto ……121
Jusanya [boxwood comb shop] Tokyo ……30
Jusanya [boxwood comb shop] Kyoto ……129

(K)

Kadomasa [restaurant] Takayama ……76
Kagetsu [restaurant] Nagasaki ……176
Kagi [noodle shop] Izumo ……160
Kagizen Yoshifusa [sweets shop] Kyoto ……122
Kaisaku [restaurant] Shizuoka ……81
Kakiden [restaurant] Kyoto ……102
Kamesuehiro [sweets shop] Kyoto ……119
Kameya [sweets shop] Kawagoe ……46
Kameya Iori [sweets shop] Kyoto ……117
Kameya Kiyonaga [sweets shop] Kyoto ……117
Kameya Mutsu [sweets shop] Kyoto ……117
Kameya Yoshinaga [sweets shop] Kyoto ……117
Kamishige [fishmeat dumpling shop] Tokyo ……34
Kanaizumi [noodle shop] Takamatsu ……162
Kaneda [restaurant] Tokyo ……37
Kano [dyeing & weaving shop] Kyoto ……93
Karako [teahouse] Takayama ……73
Kashiwaya [musical instruments shop] Tokyo ……33
Kawabata Doki [sweets shop] Kyoto ……116
Kawabata Seihachi [restaurant] Yonago ……157
Kawabun [restaurant] Nagoya ……82
Kawajiri Brewery [*sake* brewer] Takayama ……75
Kawakami [sweets, teahouse] Kyoto ……126
Kawamichiya Misokaan [noodle shop] Kyoto ……108
Kawamichiya Sohonke [sweets shop] Kyoto ……118
Kawasaki [paper shop] Kyoto ……127
Kawasho [*sushi* shop] Fukuoka ……169
Kazariya [rice cake shop] Kyoto ……125
Kichikudo [bamboo-work shop] Kyoto ……127
Kifuji [restaurant] Kyoto ……100
Kigaru [noodle shop] Mastue ……168
Kikkodo [sweets shop] Kurashiki ……155
Kikunoi [restaurant] Kyoto ……102
Kikuya [teahouse] Tokyo ……44
Kikuya [sweets shop] Yamato Koriyama ……142
Kikyoya [inn] Magome ……64
Kinchikudo [cosmetic shop] Kyoto ……129
Kinkoan [rice dumpling shop] Kyoto ……126
Kita Brewery [*sake* brewer] Nonoichi ……56
Kita Family [memorial hall] Nonoichi ……57
Kitamura [restaurant] Osaka ……144
Kitaro [restaurant] Kyoto ……109
Kitcho [restaurant] Osaka ……143
Kiyomizu Rokubei [pottery] Kyoto ……86
Kobaien [*sumi* ink shop] Nara ……135
Kobian [restaurant] Osaka ……146
Koeido Takeda [dumpling shop] Okayama 154
Kogetsu [sweets shop] Kyoto ……124
Kogetsu [sweets shop] Nara ……140
Komagata Dojo [restaurant] Tokyo ……38
Komatsutei [teahouse] Takamatsu ……162
Konaya Kotaro [noodle shop] Yonezawa ……22
Konjaku [indigo goods shop] Kyoto ……130
Konohana [*sake* brewery] Aizu Wakamatsu ……26
Konomien [tea shop] Yanagawa ……170
Koshinzuka [inn] Tsumago ……66
Kososhi [noodle shop] Matsue ……158
Kotoriya [*kimono* shop] Takayama ……76
Kototoi Dango [dumpling shop] Tokyo ……43
Kume [old family] Yashima ……163
Kuremutsu [pub, restaurant] Tokyo ……39
Kusakabe Family [folk art museum] Takayama ……68
Kutsuwado Soke [sweets shop] Takamatsu ……162
Kyo Horiya [doll shop] Kyoto ……128
Kyotomi [inn, restaurant] Yamato Koriyama ……142
Kyugetsu [sweets shop] Tokyo ……43

(M)

Mamemasa [sweets shop] Kyoto ……121
Manjuya [comb shop] Yabuhara ……67
Mankamero [restaurant] Kyoto ……101
Manmando [sweets shop] Nara ……140
Maruokaya [miller] Kanazawa ……48
Marusan Hompo [dyeing shop] Kyoto ……131
Masuda Tokubei [*sake* brewer] Kyoto ……114
Matsukawaya [inn, restaurant] Saga ……171
Matsumaeya [*konbu* shop] Kyoto ……110
Matsumoto [*kimono* shop] Tokyo ……31
Matsumoto [restaurant] Osaka ……148
Matsumoto Mingeikan [folk art museum] Matsumoto ……78
Matsuya [sweets shop] Fukuoka ……168
Matsuya Tobei [sweets shop] Kyoto ……120
Matsuzaki Senbei [rice cracker shop] Tokyo ……43

Meotozenzai [sweets, teahouse] Osaka……152
Michikusa [restaurant] Tokyo ……………………41
Mimasuya [sweets shop] Tokyo ………………45
Mimiu [restaurant] Osaka……………………146
Minochu [sweets shop] Nagoya ………………83
Minokichi [restaurant] Kyoto ………………100
Minoko [restaurant] Kyoto …………………101
Mitsutaya [*miso* shop] Aizu Wakamatsu …26
Miyaken [restaurant] Nagoya ………………82
Miyaoka Machikan [general shop] Kawagoe ……………………………………46
Miyawaki Baisen'an [fan shop] Kyoto ……87
Mochitomi [rice cake shop] Kanazawa ……50
Mori Brewery [*sake* brewer] Kurashiki ……154
Morihachi [sweets shop] Kanazawa ………50
Mori Narazuke [pickle shop] Nara ………139
Moroeya [sweets shop] Kanazawa …………51
Moroeya [sweets shop] Kanazawa …………58
Murakamiju [pickle shop] Kyoto …………112
Mutsumi [restaurant] Kyoto ………………107
Myokoen [tea shop] Nagoya…………………82
(N)
Nagatoya [sweets shop] Aizu Wakamatsu………25
Nakae [restaurant] Tokyo……………………40
Nakahata [restaurant] Kyoto ………………96
Nakamiya [old family] Kanazawa …………60
Nakamura [restaurant] Kyoto………………106
Nakamuraro Niken-jaya [restaurant] Kyoto ……98
Nakanishi Hakataori [weaver] Fukuoka …168
Nakanoya [folkcraft shop] Takayama ……77
Nakasei [restaurant] Tokyo…………………37
Nakaya [druggist] Kanazawa ………………49
Nakayama [doll shop] Kyoto ………………128
Nakazato [restaurant] Kyoto ………………96
Naniwa Zenzai [sweets, teahouse] Osaka………152
Naraya [sweets shop] Aizu Shiokawa ……28
Narita [pickle shop] Kyoto …………………112
Narumiya [sweets shop] Kitakata …………28
Niki Brewery [*sake* brewer] Takayama ……74
Ninben [dried bonito shop] Tokyo …………34
Noguchi [*kimono* shop] Kyoto ………………91
Notoya [sweets, teahouse] Takayama ……73
(O)
Obiya Sutematsu [*kimono* shop] Kyoto ……92
Ogawa [old family] Kanazawa………………61
Oguraya Yamamoto [*konbu* shop] Osaka …149
Ohara shinise [sweets shop] Karatsu ……172
Ohiyaki [pottery] Kanazawa…………………54
Oida Brewery [*sake* brewer] Takayama……75
Oiwake Yokan [sweets shop] Shimizu ……80
Okakane [fabric shop] Arimatsu……………82
Okakei [*kimono* shop] Kyoto ………………89
Okakimi [*kimono* shop] Kyoto………………130
Okutan [restaurant] Kyoto …………………109
Omasa [restaurant] Kyoto……………………96
Omodakaya [folk art museum] Gujo Hachiman …………………………………78
Onoya [*tabi* shop] Tokyo ……………………30
Onoya [teahouse] Takayama ………………72
Onoya [*miso* shop] Takayama………………74
Osada [indigo-goods shop] Izumo …………160
Osakaya [sweets shop] Tokyo ………………42
Osawa [tea shop] Tokyo ……………………36
Osawa [restaurant] Kyoto……………………97
Ota [old family] Kakunodate ………………18
Otomoro [restaurant] Kanazawa……………55
Otora [fishcake shop] Osaka………………148
Otsu Kamaboko [fishcake shop] Yanagawa ……………………………………170
Owariya [noodle shop] Kyoto ………………108
(R)
Raku Kichizaemon [pottery] Kyoto ………86
Rakugan Bunko [data room] Kanazawa …51
Rengyokuan [noodle shop] Tokyo …………37
Ryuguchiya Korekiyo [sweets shop] Nagoya ……………………………………83
(S)
Saami [restaurant] Kamakura ………………46
Saito Kisukedo [dyeing shop] Ugo Honjo …19
Sakaguchiya [inn] Takayama ………………69
Sakuraiya [dumpling shop] Kyoto …………125
Sakuramamiya [cinnamon candy shop] Gujo Hachiman ……………………………78
Sakuramochi Honke [sweets shop] Kyoto………126
Sanmachi [folkcraft shop] Takayama ……77
Sanshibo [pottery shop] Kyoto ……………132
Sanuki Mingeikan [folk art museum] Takamatsu……………………………………162
Sanuki Udon [noodle shop] Takamatsu …163
Sasanoyuki [restaurant] Tokyo ……………40
Sasau [*kimono* shop] Kyoto ………………90
Sasaya Iori [sweets shop] Kyoto …………118
Sato [paper shop] Onomichi ………………157
Sekibeya [rice cake shop] Shizuoka ………80
Senmaruya [*yuba* shop] Kyoto ……………113
Shichimiya [spice shop] Kyoto……………114
Shimizu Kintsuba [sweets, teahouse] Tokyo ……44
Shimokamo Saryo [restaurant] Kyoto ……100
Shinkawa [noodle shop] Kurashiki ………155
Shinmiura [restaurant] Fukuoka……………169
Shinya [rice cake shop] Tsumago …………65
Shioyoshiken [sweets shop] Kyoto…………123
Shiramasa [antique art shop] Takayama …76
Shirayukido Etsuzan [rice cake shop] Yanagawa ……………………………………170
Shiruko [restaurant] Kyoto ………………106
Shirusei [restaurant] Osaka………………152
Shobentangotei [restaurant] Osaka ………147
Shogetsu [inn, restaurant] Yanagawa ……170
Shorankyo [inn, restaurant] Kyoto ………100
Shuetsu [pickle shop] Tokyo ………………36
Shutoen [pottery shop] Kurashiki…………156
Somotaro [*okonomiyaki* shop] Tokyo ………45
Sugukiya Rokurobei [pickle shop] Kyoto …113

Sumiya [restaurant] Kyoto ……94
Sumiyoshi [inn] Takayama ……69
Surugaya Shimozato [sweets shop] Kyoto ……121
Susaki [restaurant] Takayama ……76
Sushiman [*sushi* shop] Osaka ……145
Suzuki [iron cauldron shop] Morioka ……20
Suzukiya Rihei [lacquerware shop] Aizu Wakamatsu ……24
Suzumeodori Sohonke [sweets shop] Nagoya ……83
(T)
Tachibanaya [teahouse] Tokyo ……44
Tachibanaya Juei [sweets shop] Osaka ……150
Tachikichi [pottery shop] Kyoto ……130
Taigetsu [restaurant] Shizuoka Maruko ……81
Tajikaya [teahouse] Takayama ……72
Tajimaya [inn] Magome ……64
Takagi [malted rice shop] Kanazawa ……48
Takahashi [tea shop] Yonago ……157
Takasebune [pub, restaurant] Kyoto ……107
Takefuji [bamboo-work shop] Aizu Wakamatsu ……25
Takezono Ornament shop [gold & silver-work shop] Kanazawa ……54
Takino [restaurant] Aizu Wakamatsu ……28
Takoume [restaurant] Osaka ……147
Tamakiya [*tsukudani* shop] Tokyo ……34
Tamanoya [restaurant] Kyoto ……101
Tanakacho [*mirinzuke* shop] Kyoto ……113
Tanbaya [antique art shop] Kyoto ……131
Tatsumi [dyeing & weaving shop] Kyoto ……93
Tatsuno [tatami shop] Kanazawa ……58
Tawaraya [candy shop] Kanazawa ……52
Tawaraya [inn] Kyoto ……97
Tawaraya Yoshitomi [sweets shop] Kyoto ……120
Tenpyodo [antique art shop] Kyoto ……132
Tenyasu [*tsukudani* shop] Tokyo ……35
Terashima Sohonten [sweets shop] Osaka ……150
Tochiori Dye shop [Kaga Yuzen silk shop] Kanazawa ……54
Tokkuriya [inn (data room)] Narai ……67
Tokugetsu [pickle shop] Nagoya ……82
Tomatsuya [fan shop] Kyoto ……128
Tomishiro [restaurant] Kyoto ……95
Tomoegata [restaurant] Tokyo ……41
Tono-chaya [restaurant] Nara ……138
Toraya [inn] Kotohira ……164
Toraya Kurokawa [sweets shop] Kyoto ……123
Torishin [restaurant] Kyoto ……104
Toriyasa [restaurant] Kyoto ……104
Tosahan [restaurant] Kochi ……166
Tsuboi Flag & Streamer Shop [dyeing shop] Gujo Hachiman ……79
Tsuchiya [inn] Tsumago ……67
Tsuchiya [sweets, teahouse] Narai ……67
Tsuda Mizuhiki [paper cord shop] Kanazawa ……54
Tsujitome [restaurant] Kyoto ……99
Tsumugiya Kichibei [dyeing & weaving, *kimono* shop] Tokyo ……33
Tsunosei [sweets shop] Osaka ……151
Tsuruizutsu [restaurant] Aizu Wakamatsu 27
Tsuruya [sweets shop] Saga ……171
Tsuruya Hachiman [sweets shop] Osaka ……150
Tsuruya Yoshinobu [sweets shop] Kyoto ……118
Tsutaya [restaurant] Kyoto ……99
(U)
Ubagamochi Yorotei [teahouse] Kusatsu ……134
Uchihoya [candle shop, memorial hall] Takayama ……70
Uoju [caterer] Tokyo ……41
Usagiya [sweets shop] Tokyo ……42
Utsugi [dyeing & weaving shop] Kyoto ……92
(W)
Wachigaiya [restaurant] Kyoto ……94
Warajiya [restaurant] Kyoto ……105
Waraya [noodle shop] Yashima ……163
Watanabe [dyeing shop] Gujo Hachiman ……79
Watanabe Seikodo [paper hanger] Takayama ……77
Watarai brewery [*sake* brewer] Tsuruoka Oyama ……21
(Y)
Yabu Soba [noodle shop] Tokyo ……37
Yagumo Honjin [inn, restaurant] Shinji ……159
Yamabana Heihachi [restaurant] Kyoto ……98
Yamabana Sokyudo [sweets shop] Kyoto ……126
Yamadaichi [rice cake shop] Shizuoka ……80
Yamagiri [restaurant] Tsumago ……66
Yamaguchi gen [*kimono* shop] Kyoto ……88
Yamamoto Nori [*nori* shop] Tokyo ……36
Yamasho [dyeing & weaving shop] Kyoto ……93
Yamatoya [restaurant] Osaka ……144
Yanagi-chaya [restaurant] Nara ……138
Yano [dried food shop] Yonago ……157
Yaoi [pickle shop] Kyoto ……113
Yaosan [*miso* shop] Kyoto ……110
Yashirojin [*kimono* shop] Kyoto ……88
Yasushige [cutlery shop] Kyoto ……131
Yatsuhashi Nishio [sweets shop] Kyoto ……122
Yomogiya [inn, folkcraft shop] Magome ……64
Yonoya [comb shop] Tokyo ……30
Yoshijima Family [folk art museum] Takayama ……68
Yoshikawa [inn, restaurant] Kyoto ……106
Yosso [restaurant] Nagasaki ……174
Yoyokaku [inn, restaurant] Higashi Karatsu ……173
Yubahan [teahouse] Kyoto ……111
Yumeido [teahouse] Nara ……141
Yuranosuke [restaurant] Kyoto ……107
(Z)
Zeitakuame Honpo [bean confectionary] Nara ……140